Table of Contents

"The Most Difficult Puzzles Ever Devised"

Charles Best, one of the pioneers in the search for a cure for diabetes, once explained what it is about medical research that intrigued him so. "It's not just the gratification of knowing one is helping people," he confided, "although that probably is a more heroic and selfless motivation. Those feelings may enter in, but truly, what I find best is the feeling of going toe to toe with nature, of trying to solve the most difficult puzzles ever devised. The answers are there somewhere, those keys that will solve the puzzle and make the patient well. But how will those keys be found?"

Since the dawn of civilization, nothing has so puzzled people—and often frightened them, as well—as the onset of illness in a body or mind that had seemed healthy before. A seizure, the inability of a heart to pump, the sudden deterioration of muscle tone in a small child—being unable to reverse such conditions or even to understand why they occur was unspeakably frustrating to healers. Even before there were names for such conditions, even before they were understood at all, each was a reminder of how complex the human body was, and how vulnerable.

DISEASES & DISORDERS

COPD

Melissa Abramovitz

LUCENT BOOKS
A part of Gale, Cengage Learning

GALE
CENGAGE Learning

Farmington Hills, Mich • San Francisco • New York • Waterville, Maine
Meriden, Conn • Mason, Ohio • Chicago

GALE
CENGAGE Learning™

LIBRARY OF CONGRESS CATALOGING-IN-PUBLICATION DATA

Abramovitz, Melissa, 1954-
  COPD / by Melissa Abramovitz.
    pages cm. -- (Diseases and disorders)
  Summary: "This title in Lucent Diseases and Disorders series focus on COPD and details how it is the third leading cause of death in the United States. It is often a disease of shame and blame since it is more often than not caused by smoking. COPD is often under-di_ _ ~ed and under-treated. The books goes on to detail how the disease impacts the patient, the care givers, what treatment options are available, and what the future holds for people afflicted with COPD"-- Provided by publisher.
  Includes bibliographical references and index.
  ISBN 978-1-4205-1239-7 (hardback)
  1. Lungs--Diseases, Obstructive--Juvenile literature. I. Title.
  RC776.O3A27 2015
  616.2'4--dc23
                                                          2014035351

Lucent Books
27500 Drake Rd.
Farmington Hills, MI 48331

ISBN-13: 978-1-4205-1239-7
ISBN-10: 1-4205-1239-0

Printed in the United States of America
1 2 3 4 5 6 7 19 18 17 16 15

While our grappling with understanding diseases has been frustrating at times, it has also provided some of humankind's most heroic accomplishments. Alexander Fleming's accidental discovery in 1928 of a mold that could be turned into penicillin has resulted in the saving of untold millions of lives. The isolation of the enzyme insulin has reversed what was once a death sentence for anyone with diabetes. There have been great strides in combating conditions for which there is not yet a cure, too. Medicines can help AIDS patients live longer, diagnostic tools such as mammography and ultrasounds can help doctors find tumors while they are treatable, and laser surgery techniques have made the most intricate, minute operations routine.

This "toe-to-toe" competition with diseases and disorders is even more remarkable when seen in a historical continuum. An astonishing amount of progress has been made in a very short time. Just two hundred years ago, the existence of germs as a cause of some diseases was unknown. In fact, it was less than 150 years ago that a British surgeon named Joseph Lister had difficulty persuading his fellow doctors that washing their hands before delivering a baby might increase the chances of a healthy delivery (especially if they had just attended to a diseased patient)!

Each book in Lucent's Diseases and Disorders series explores a disease or disorder and the knowledge that has been accumulated (or discarded) by doctors through the years. Each book also examines the tools used for pinpointing a diagnosis, as well as the various means that are used to treat or cure a disease. Finally, new ideas are presented—techniques or medicines that may be on the horizon.

Frustration and disappointment are still part of medicine, for not every disease or condition can be cured or prevented. But the limitations of knowledge are being pushed outward constantly; the "most difficult puzzles ever devised" are finding challengers every day.

Shame and Blame

Although chronic obstructive pulmonary disease (COPD) is the third leading cause of death in the United States and affects more than 24 million people in the United States alone, it is widely underdiagnosed and undertreated. In addition, many people throughout the world are unaware of what COPD is, and research is vastly underfunded. COPD involves impaired breathing from progressively worsening blockages in the breathing tubes (*chronic* means "long term," *obstructive* means "blockage," and *pulmonary* refers to the lungs).

Experts believe the lack of awareness and other disparities result from the fact that 75 to 90 percent of COPD cases are caused by smoking. In turn, patients tend to blame themselves for their illness and are stigmatized by their families and society as well. Robert Edwards of the Australian Lung Foundation explains that "COPD has been an afterthought for decades, largely neglected by pharmaceutical companies, researchers and government with healthcare dollars to spend. . . . Many sufferers have felt guilty and isolated by their disease because it carries the stigma of being self-inflicted."[1]

Indeed, COPD does not inspire the sympathy or public support that many other diseases do. As a 2013 *New York Times* article points out, "You don't see supermarket products emblazoned with ribbons to help support research on chronic obstructive pulmonary disease. Major corporations don't sponsor walkathons for thousands of cheering supporters."[2]

Paradoxically, studies indicate that widespread awareness of the dangers of smoking and laws prohibiting smoking in public places have inadvertently worsened the stigma associated with COPD. For many years patients informally reported that antismoking efforts heightened this stigma. Then a 2011 study reported in the *Scandinavian Journal of Caring Science* verified that nonsmoking enforcement led people with COPD to feel even more "exiled in the world of the healthy, because of self blame and society's stigmatisation. . . . The participants experienced feelings of disgrace through subtle blame and a lack of support from their social network, health care encounters and larger society."[3]

The Effects of Stigma

Many people with COPD state that the self-blame and other people's reactions to the disease are emotionally devastating. In fact, a 2010 study by researchers at Växjö University in Sweden found that COPD patients who formerly smoked said their number one concern about their disease was guilt over causing it. Patients also find the reactions of health care professionals upsetting. This is why many resist going to their doctor for diagnosis and treatment. Many patients say doctors reinforce the COPD stigma by seeming unsympathetic and expressing the belief that treatment is futile. This occurs despite the fact that effective treatments do exist for slowing the progression of the disease and improving patients' quality of life.

Some patients resist going to doctors for other stigma-related reasons. A 2012 study by Canadian researchers explains, "Some smokers with COPD may feel that they are not entitled to health care or sympathy from others, and some avoid health care visits to avoid 'preaching' about smoking."[4] Indeed, some COPD patients do not think they can stop smoking or do not wish to, and they know doctors will tell them to do so.

The reactions of people other than doctors also cause patients anxiety. As COPD patient Fabiana Talbot writes on the COPD Foundation website:

> The dreaded question for individuals living with COPD is "Did you smoke?" So much is insinuated in three simple words, and so many in our community have to withstand the stigma associated with the disease. All too often, people with COPD are afraid to reach out for help, let alone raise awareness for the disease, because they believe in the end they will be shamed and blamed for smoking.[5]

Stigma also keeps many patients from going out in public or from complying with parts of their treatment plans. For instance, many who need oxygen refuse to use their oxygen tanks and nose cannulae (flexible plastic tubes that feed oxygen into the nose) when they are outside their homes. One patient who participated in a study about treatment compliance stated that she did not use oxygen away from home because "I think I feel like it's shameful because I have to do it because I smoked."[6]

Some patients, on the other hand, do not allow shame to govern their lives. A patient named Mike McBride explains how he ignores stigma and forges ahead to live fully within the constraints of COPD: "I refuse to stay indoors or hide because I have to take oxygen with me wherever I go. My life experience says that I would rather you feel awkward because you find my appearance distasteful, than me hide indoors and miss the great and wonderful things God intended for me to be a part of."[7] McBride enjoys walking in marathons for people with disabilities. He carries his oxygen tanks in a backpack or in a wheeled cart he designed. His support crew of friends helps out by meeting him every few miles to give him fresh oxygen tanks.

Improvement Efforts

Stigma still impairs many patients, however, and in recent years COPD support foundations, governments, and researchers have been working on diminishing stigma and increasing

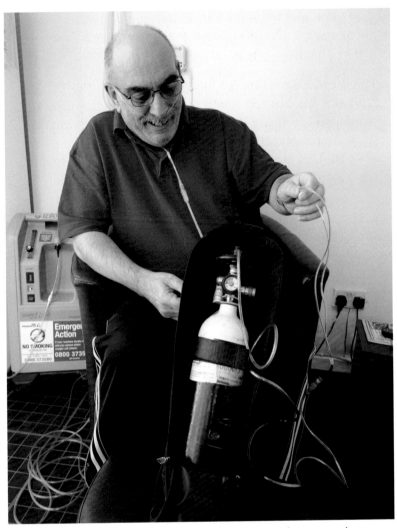

An elderly patient with COPD receives oxygen therapy at home. In the United States, the direct costs of caring for people with COPD total about $29.5 billion per year.

awareness and research for the disease. This is partly because 210 million people in the world are estimated to have COPD, and experts have realized the economic and personal toll is staggering. In the United States the direct costs of caring for people with COPD total about $29.5 billion per year. The indirect costs are about $20.4 billion. Indirect costs include the loss of productivity and reduced income earned by patients when they are sick. COPD often strikes people during the prime of their lives—between ages forty and sixty—when they are raising families, working, and leading active lives. They must often retire from their jobs, and the financial and emotional toll for families is significant. For the many older people with COPD, the disease can make their final years unpleasant and take away their independence.

Programs like the National Heart, Lung, and Blood Institute's (NHLBI's) Learn More Breathe Better® program have done much to improve awareness, prevention, diagnosis, treatment, and research. November is now National COPD Awareness Month, and awareness of COPD has improved significantly. In 2004, for example, only 49 percent of American adults had heard of COPD. In 2013 an NHLBI survey found this was up to 65 percent. U.S. lawmakers have also responded to advocacy group efforts by mandating that Medicare pay for pulmonary rehabilitation (PR) treatment programs. Despite these improvements, however, experts say there is still a long way to go before the stigma associated with COPD declines and people with the disease seek and benefit from vastly improved treatments. As James Kiley of the NHLBI notes in a National Institutes of Health news article, "COPD is the only major chronic disease where deaths are not decreasing."[8]

CHAPTER ONE

What Is COPD?

COPD actually refers to a group of lung diseases. As the COPD Foundation explains, "COPD is an umbrella term used to describe progressive lung diseases including emphysema, chronic bronchitis, refractory (non-reversible) asthma, and some forms of bronchiectasis. This disease is characterized by increasing breathlessness."[9]

Although COPD was not formally described until the 1600s, experts believe it has affected people throughout human history. According to the book *Physiologic Basis of Respiratory Disease*, "COPD is a very old disease, perhaps one of the oldest lung diseases ever suffered."[10] Anthropologists have evidence that COPD occurred in Egyptian mummies two thousand to thirty-five hundred years old. These mummies' lungs have blackened areas called anthracotic pigments and are swollen, which is characteristic of lungs affected by COPD.

In 1972 three Eskimo hunters found another ancient mummified body with evidence of COPD on St. Lawrence Island in the Bering Sea. Anthropologists in Fairbanks, Alaska, examined the frozen woman's body and determined it was more than sixteen hundred years old. The lungs had signs of airway narrowing and emphysema (enlarged or burst air sacs)—hallmark signs of COPD. The lungs were also anthracotic.

First References to COPD

The first known medical reference to COPD and the conditions that underlie it appeared in 1679, when the Swiss physician Theophilus Bonet used the words "voluminous lungs"[11] to describe the condition of a patient with what is now known as emphysema. The word *emphysema* comes from the Greek term *physe*, which means "to blow into." *Emphysema* has come to mean "inflated with air," because the air sacs, or alveoli, in people with emphysema are enlarged. In 1814 the British physician Charles Badham described another characteristic condition seen in COPD—excess mucus in the airways and a chronic cough. He called the condition catarrh. Catarrh is now referred to as chronic bronchitis.

The French doctor René Laënnec synthesized the chronic bronchitis and emphysema elements of chronic lung disease when he wrote the first detailed description of how the lungs of people with these conditions do not properly remove air and mucus: "In opening the chest, it is not unusual to find that the lungs do not collapse, but they fill up the cavity completely on each side of the heart. . . . The bronchus of the trachea [windpipe] are often at the same time a good deal filled with mucous fluid."[12]

After Laënnec linked emphysema and chronic bronchitis to one another, doctors still did not clearly define the conditions that make up COPD until 1965. Before this time, physicians referred to related conditions like emphysema and chronic bronchitis as chronic obstructive bronchopulmonary disease, chronic airflow obstruction, or chronic obstructive lung disease. In 1965 William Briscoe of Columbia University used the term *chronic obstructive pulmonary disease* for the first time to describe the constellation of progressive lung conditions that often coexist. Most COPD patients have emphysema and chronic bronchitis, but some do not have both conditions. Some have other conditions like bronchiectasis (abnormally stretched and widened airways) as well.

The Respiratory System

The conditions that underlie COPD involve progressively worsening lung damage that makes breathing increasingly difficult. The progressive nature of the disease makes it especially devastating because a functioning respiratory, or pulmonary, system is essential for sustaining life. One of the main functions of the respiratory system is to bring in oxygen from the air so

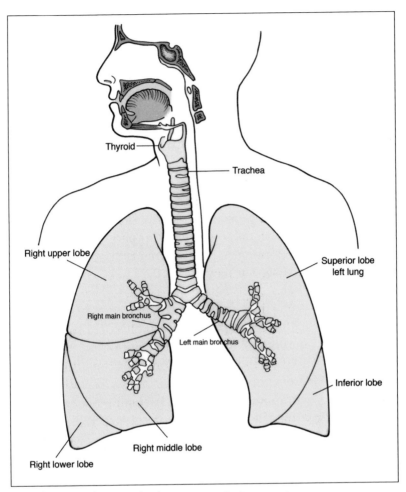

This drawing depicts the human respiratory system.

the bloodstream can carry the oxygen to body cells. The other major function is to rid the body of the carbon dioxide waste products that result from cells burning oxygen for fuel.

The respiratory system starts inside the mouth and nose. Humans breathe in air through these organs. Mucous membranes that line the nose and mouth moisten and warm the air as it passes through. Mucus and tiny hairs called cilia in the nose trap particles such as pollen and smoke and usually push them outward or send them to the digestive system. Sometimes, though, these particles proceed past the next airway structures, the pharynx (throat), larynx (voice box), and trachea. After passing through the pharynx, larynx, and trachea, the air, which contains about 21 percent oxygen, enters the bronchial tubes, or bronchi. Bronchi also contain mucous membranes that produce mucus to trap particles and cilia that push particles and mucus outward. Bronchi branch into smaller tubes called bronchioles. At the end of each bronchiole is a cluster of alveoli. Healthy adult lungs each contain about 300 million alveoli. These air sacs have thin walls about as thick as soap bubbles. Oxygen

Other Effects of COPD

COPD can affect many parts of the body besides the lungs. Breathlessness that leads to a lack of physical activity increases the risk of muscle wasting and osteoporosis (thinning bones). Muscle wasting and osteoporosis make it even more difficult for people to move around and exercise. In turn, this further weakens the lungs.

The breathing difficulties and oxygen deficiency seen in COPD often affect the heart as well. People who must work harder to breathe often overcompensate by working the heart harder. This leads to an enlarged, weakened heart. A weakened heart does not pump efficiently, and fluid may build up around it, leading to congestive heart failure and worsening breathing difficulties.

Many people with COPD also have cognitive and emotional problems. A study reported in March 2014 in the *Journal of the American Medical Association* found that older people with COPD experience significantly more problems with planning, attention, and problem solving than those without COPD. Researchers are attempting to determine whether inadequate amounts of oxygen in the brain are contributing to these impairments. An alternative hypothesis is that many people with COPD sleep poorly, and too little sleep impairs mental functions.

from the air in the alveoli slips through the alveolar walls and enters the small blood vessels, or capillaries, in the lungs. A substance called hemoglobin in red blood cells then carries oxygen throughout the body.

While oxygen is passing from alveoli into capillaries in the lungs, carbon dioxide is going from the blood in the capillaries into the alveoli to be exhaled through the nose and mouth. The process by which oxygen and carbon dioxide enter and exit the alveoli is known as gas exchange, since oxygen and carbon

Indeed, many COPD patients wake up frequently due to sleep apnea. Individuals with sleep apnea stop breathing while asleep, often hundreds of times per night. The condition can be fatal and is especially dangerous when combined with COPD.

Elderly people with COPD experience additional, related problems involving attention, planning, and problem solving.

dioxide are both gases. During the gas exchange process, the alveoli, which can stretch like balloons, inflate when air enters them. They then deflate when carbon dioxide is being exhaled. A muscle underneath the lungs called the diaphragm pulls and pushes on the lungs to power these inhalations and exhalations. Muscles in the bronchi contribute to air transport as well.

Poor Lung Function

The gas exchange process is critical for health and life. If the lungs do not take in adequate amounts of oxygen or do not exhale adequate amounts of carbon dioxide, the body can become too acidic or too alkaline to survive. Over-acidity from too much carbon dioxide is known as respiratory acidosis. Over-alkalinity from abnormally low levels of carbon dioxide is called respiratory alkalosis. In order to prevent these conditions, the lungs must be able to stretch and return to their normal size to take in air and breathe out carbon dioxide.

Damage to various parts of the lungs leads to difficulties with performing different aspects of the respiratory process. For example, when cilia in the airways are damaged, mucus accumulates and blocks air from flowing. Mucus buildup and irritation from harmful particles can also lead to airway swelling, or inflammation, that impacts the ability to push air in and carbon dioxide out. In emphysema the damage to alveoli robs them of their ability to stretch, and they often break. This results in fewer, larger alveoli. The Mayo Clinic website explains, "As it worsens, emphysema turns the spherical air sacs—clustered like bunches of grapes—into large, irregular pockets with gaping holes in their inner walls. This reduces the surface area of the lungs and, in turn, the amount of oxygen that reaches your bloodstream."[13] With fewer, damaged alveoli, inadequate gas exchange occurs. Emphysema also weakens the bronchioles, which then collapse when an individual exhales. Thus, air that should be exhaled becomes trapped in the lungs.

The combination of emphysema and chronic bronchitis that occurs in most cases of COPD leads to the characteristic symptoms. The American Thoracic Society explains that the main difficulty experienced by COPD patients is emptying air out of the lungs: "This difficulty in emptying air out of the lungs (airflow obstruction) can lead to shortness of breath or feeling tired because you are working harder to breathe."[14] As lung damage grows worse, COPD symptoms also worsen.

COPD Symptoms

The most common symptoms of COPD are increasing breathlessness (also known as dyspnea), coughing, and a feeling of tightness in the chest. A patient named Susie Bowers describes her initial symptoms: "I began to have spells when I couldn't catch my breath while doing the simplest of activities."[15]

For some individuals, the first indications of COPD occur when another chronic condition such as asthma seems to worsen. For example, a patient named Don Davis had asthma,

For some individuals, the first indication of their COPD occurs when another chronic condition, such as asthma, seems to worsen.

which involves airway inflammation, all his life and noticed he was getting out of breath more quickly than usual at age forty. "I told the doctor I thought my asthma was changing. She realized there was more to it than that,"[16] he told the Alpha-1 Foundation. Tests indicated that Davis did indeed have COPD.

Many people do not even notice symptoms of COPD in its early stages. Some notice them but believe breathlessness is an ordinary part of aging. Although lung function does decline somewhat with age, doctors emphasize that severe breathing difficulties are not at all normal. They emphasize that anyone with breathlessness should see a physician. According to the COPD Foundation, although the lung damage seen in COPD cannot be reversed, "early screening can identify COPD before major loss of lung function occurs."[17]

Difficulties in Diagnosis

Most cases of COPD, however, are not diagnosed in the early stages for a variety of reasons. One reason is that patients avoid seeking medical help because of the stigma associated with the disease. Another reason, according to the American Lung Association, is that "people mistakenly believe that the disease is not life-threatening."[18] For women, still another reason is that COPD was historically a man's disease because fewer women smoked. Today, as more and more female smokers age, COPD affects just as many women as men. But some doctors still fail to diagnose the disease in women because they do not expect women to be affected.

The fact that other diseases can include airflow obstruction and inflammation also contributes to difficulties in diagnosing COPD. Asthma, for example, includes these characteristics, and many people with COPD are initially diagnosed with asthma. The fact that some people with COPD also have asthma makes distinguishing the two especially difficult. Asthma, however, involves reversible airway obstruction, unlike the irreversible obstruction in COPD.

In one case doctors diagnosed twenty-four-year-old Jean McCathern with asthma and allergies to pollen, dust mites, mold, and cats when she began experiencing breathing problems in 1980. McCathern, who was in the U.S. Air Force, followed her doctors' recommendations to give away her cat, take allergy shots, and start a new career so she would not have to travel throughout the world. Her condition did not improve, and it was not until 2004 that a pulmonologist (a physician who specializes in lung diseases) determined that she had a form of COPD known as alpha-1 antitrypsin deficiency. Unfortunately, this type of misdiagnosis is common because "most doctors don't even think about the [correct] diagnosis,"[19] allergist Timothy Craig of the Penn State Hershey Medical Center told the *Washington Post*. The fact that McCathern never smoked also contributed to her doctors' initial reluctance to test for COPD. The twenty-year delay in determining the correct diagnosis allowed McCathern's condition to advance to the point that she developed severe emphysema and bronchiectasis.

Spirometry

Diagnosing COPD is not technically difficult, and experts lament the fact that many physicians are not aware of a simple test called spirometry that quickly achieves this goal. Spirometry uses a machine called the spirometer, which the British surgeon John Hutchison invented in 1846. An individual blows the air out of his or her lungs into the mouthpiece of this simple device to allow doctors to measure the lungs' forced vital capacity—the maximum amount of air a person can breathe out after taking a deep breath.

Hutchison also developed methods of comparing people's expected lung capacity. This allowed doctors to determine how much air a person of a certain height, weight, sex, and age should be able to force out of the lungs. These expected values turned out to be consistent enough over time that doctors later figured out how to use them to assess whether a particular patient had COPD or whether the disease was worsening. When Hutchison presented his findings in a presentation to the British Royal Society, he explained, "So constant is this deep expiratory power, or quantity of air expired [exhaled], that I

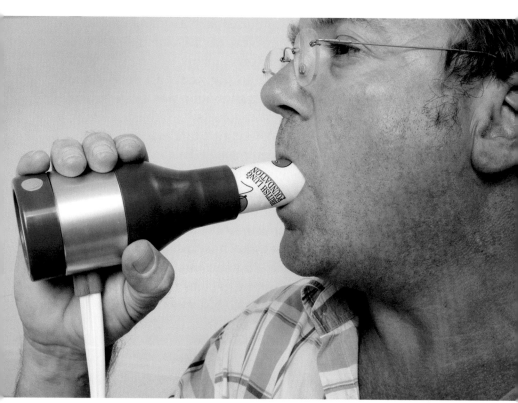

A man uses a spirometer to check his lung efficiency.

have frequently found adults eighteen months or two years afterwards breathe within two or three cubic inches of the original quantity. I have blown into this instrument hundreds of times, and yet I cannot exceed the original quantity determined five years ago."[20]

Hutchison's spirometer was a huge step forward in giving doctors the primary diagnostic tool for COPD, but it was not until 1947 that the French doctors Robert Tiffeneau and André Pinelli introduced the concept of timing patients' vital capacity to obtain a true picture of how well their lungs were functioning. The index used today to diagnose COPD is called the Tiffeneau-Pinelli index. This index is the ratio of two numbers the spirometer calculates—the amount of air the person blows out of the lungs in the first second and the amount he or she blows out after six or more seconds. The first number is known as FEV1, or the forced expiratory volume in the first second. The second number is called FEV6 or FVC (the forced vital capacity), which is the total amount of air exhaled after six seconds. FEV1 and FVC are identical in healthy people. However, people with COPD take longer to exhale a breath of air, so the numbers differ.

Spirometers measure FEV1 and FVC in liters, and their ratio is expressed as a percentage of the predicted value for an individual of a particular age, sex, height, and sometimes ethnicity (most measurement scales do not include ethnicity). Most experts consider a normal FEV1/FVC ratio to be between .75 and .8. Values under .7, or 70 percent of the predicted value, indicate obstructed airflow and COPD—except in elderly people, who may have values between .65 and .7 without having COPD.

Doctors assign COPD patients a disease stage based on their FEV1/FVC ratio. The longer it takes an individual to completely exhale, the more severe his or her lung obstructions are, and thus the more severe his or her COPD is. The assigned stages sometimes vary according to scales formulated by different organizations, but most define people with a ratio of 60 to 69 percent of the expected value as having mild COPD, 50 to 59 percent as moderate COPD, and less than 50 percent as having severe, or end-stage, COPD.

Pulmonologists emphasize that these stages do not predict how long a COPD patient has to live or how fast the disease will progress. This varies widely among individuals. As respiratory therapist Jane M. Martin explains, many people given a diagnosis of end-stage COPD assume they do not have long to live, but this is not necessarily the case. "'You have end stage COPD . . .' is probably one of the most frightening—and confusing—things a person can hear," she writes. "The term 'end stage' is just a term."[21] Martin and other experts explain that *end-stage COPD* is simply a clinical term used to describe the most severe stage of COPD. How long a patient with end-stage COPD lives depends on numerous variables, such as how well the individual follows a treatment plan.

Using a Spirometer

The FEV1/FVC ratio can also be used to distinguish COPD from diseases like asthma. People with asthma will have a low FEV1/FVC ratio during an asthma attack, but the ratio will be near normal or normal after the person takes a fast-acting asthma medication. Doctors also use spirometry to assess how quickly COPD is progressing or how well a particular treatment is working.

Pulmonologists consider spirometry to be the most accurate, repeatable method of diagnosing COPD. For this reason they call it the "gold standard" for COPD diagnosis. Several types of spirometers are available today. Hospital lung function laboratories often have large, nonportable spirometers. Smaller desktop models or handheld models are used in doctors' offices. Experts stress that professionals who use spirometers should be trained in the correct procedure and in how to interpret the results so patients receive accurate information.

Although spirometers are inexpensive and easy to use with proper training, doctors in many places do not use them. This contributes to the widespread underdiagnosis of COPD. Underuse of spirometry is especially prevalent in developing countries. In India, for example, spirometry "is not available in most clinics, hospitals and diagnostic centres. Lack of use of spirometry contributes to over 50 percent of COPD patients being undiagnosed," explains physician Sundeep Salvi in *Express Healthcare*. Salvi also writes, "It is not the cost of the tool that is responsible, but the lack of knowledge about how to perform the test and interpret the test."[22]

In addition to performing a spirometry test, many physicians use chest X-rays or computed tomography (CT) to help with diagnosis. CT is a special type of computerized X-ray that gives three-dimensional pictures of internal organs. Chest X-rays and CT images do not actually diagnose COPD, but they can show lung damage that confirms emphysema and/or chronic bronchitis are present when a patient has multiple sources of breathing difficulties, such as having asthma or lung cancer along with

Comparing Lung Capacity

John Hutchison's experiments showed that an individual's height is especially important in determining lung capacity. Weight, age, and sex play a lesser role. Hutchison explained in an 1846 journal article, "The effect of mere height or length of body bears the most marked relation of all these modifiers to the vital capacity, so that I find, if I be allowed to take a man's height, I can tell what *quantity* of air he should breathe to constitute him a healthy individual." The taller the person is, the greater his or her lung capacity is. For instance, Hutchison found the average vital capacity for more than one thousand men from 5 feet to 5 feet 1 inch tall was 175 cubic inches (2.86L). For men 5 feet 3 inches tall, the average vital capacity was 188.5 cubic inches (3.08 L).

Weight, age, and sex also influence vital capacity. Hutchison found that the vital capacity of overweight men decreased in proportion to how overweight they were. Age-wise, people aged fifteen to thirty-five have the greatest vital capacity. Vital capacity gradually decreases in people aged thirty-five to sixty-five. Studies also find gender differences in vital capacity, though these differences vary with the age and height of the individual. In general, most studies indicate that males have higher vital capacities than women.

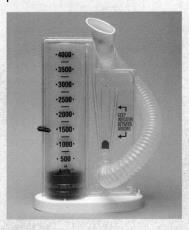

John Hutchison. "On the Capacity of the Lungs and on the Respiratory Functions, with a View of Establishing a Precise and Easy Method of Detecting Disease by the Spirometer." *Medico-Chirurgical Transactions*, vol. 29, 1846, p. 154.

A volumetric spirometer monitors lung function by measuring the maximum rate at which air is expelled from the lungs.

COPD. These images are also helpful in determining whether another disease, such as heart disease, is exacerbating COPD.

Concerns About Prevalence and Effects

Although spirometry is used much more widely in the United States than in other countries, American health officials still believe about 15 million people are unaware they have COPD. A 2014 report by the Global Initiative for Chronic Obstructive Lung Disease states, "This likely reflects the widespread under-recognition and under-diagnosis of COPD."[23] Between 12 million and 15 million Americans, on the other hand, have already been diagnosed, making COPD the most common serious lung disease in the United States.

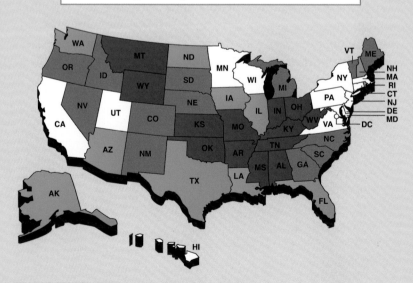

Age-Standardized Death Rate (per 100,000 U.S. population) for Chronic Obstructive Pulmonary Disease (COPD)— United States, 2010

Death Rate (per 100,000 U.S. population)
Age-Standardized

☐ 16.1–37.6   ▨ 37.7–43.3   ▨ 43.4–48.4   ■ 48.5–66.3

Taken from: Centers for Disease Control and Prevention. www.cdc.gov/copd/data.htm.

Even with widespread underdiagnosis, experts know that COPD kills about 120,000 Americans per year, making it the third leading cause of death in the United States. In 1997 a study revealed that COPD was the fourth leading cause of death. This study predicted COPD would probably become the third leading cause of death by 2020, mostly because people are living longer and the likelihood of getting COPD increases with age. However, in 2010 the Centers for Disease Control and Prevention and the National Center for Health Statistics released a report stating that COPD had become the third leading cause of death by 2008. COPD advocates used this unwelcome news to intensify efforts to encourage more widely spread early diagnosis. As John W. Walsh, president of the COPD Foundation, stated at that time, "It's unacceptable that COPD has gone from fourth to the third leading cause twelve years sooner than originally projected. This wake-up call intensifies our declaration of war on COPD."[24]

CHAPTER TWO

What Causes COPD?

One area in which scientists have made progress in understanding and attacking COPD relates to knowledge about its causes. Doctors know that progressive inflammation and damage in various parts of the lungs and airways cause the symptoms and problems associated with COPD. In turn, the root causes behind this inflammation and damage involve complex interactions between genetics, behavior, and environmental irritants.

Genetics and COPD

While cigarette smoking is known to be the strongest risk factor for COPD, it is not the only factor that plays a role in causing the disease. Not all people who smoke develop COPD—in fact, only 20 percent of smokers develop COPD—and nonsmokers also get the disease. A 2014 Global Initiative for Chronic Obstructive Lung Disease report explains that this indicates "COPD results from a gene-environment interaction."[25] This means that people who have a genetic predisposition toward lung disease and who are exposed to environments or engage in behaviors that irritate the lungs have the greatest chances of developing COPD.

Genes are the parts of deoxyribonucleic acid (DNA) molecules that code for individual traits and instruct body cells how to function. Some genetic traits are inherited directly. For example, if an individual inherits genes for brown eyes from her parents, she will have brown eyes. Some diseases, such as cystic fibrosis, are also inherited directly. If someone inherits the gene that causes cystic fibrosis, he or she will get the disease. In contrast, some traits and diseases can be inherited as a genetic predisposition. In such cases inheriting certain gene mutations makes it more likely that the individual will develop a disease like COPD if certain environmental factors or behaviors are also present.

Although cigarette smoking is the most prominent known factor that causes COPD it is not the only one.

Researchers have found that people with a genetic predisposition toward COPD show amplified inflammation—in other words, the inflammation in their lungs is worse than that seen in other people with long-term exposure to lung irritants. As the British respiratory specialist Graeme P. Currie explains in *ABC of COPD*, "All cigarette smokers have inflammatory changes within their lungs, but those who develop COPD exhibit an enhanced or abnormal inflammatory response to inhaled toxic agents."[26] In most cases this enhanced inflammation is caused by the immune system's overreacting to the presence of these irritants by producing large quantities of white blood cells that attack the foreign substances. These white blood cells also release chemicals called cytokines that increase inflammation. When this type of excessive inflammation occurs, lung cells' normal repair mechanisms cannot operate, and gradually more and more tissue is destroyed.

Alpha-1 Antitrypsin Deficiency

Different gene abnormalities that predispose certain individuals to COPD can lead to excessive lung inflammation in different ways. The most common genetic risk factor for COPD is known as alpha-1 antitrypsin deficiency (AATD). AATD is caused by mutations in genes that code for the production of alpha-1 antitrypsin (AAT) protein. The mutations cause the liver to produce abnormal AAT protein and also prevent this protein from being released into the bloodstream at a normal rate. Abnormal AAT can result in lung inflammation because the main function of AAT protein is to protect the lungs from inflammation and infection when they are exposed to inhaled irritants or infections. An AAT deficiency can therefore result in lung inflammation and other damage that lead to symptoms of COPD.

AAT protein normally protects the lungs by neutralizing, or making ineffective, an enzyme called neutrophil elastase. White blood cells in the lungs produce neutrophil elastase to destroy germs and digest damaged or aging lung cells. Neutrophil elastase is a proteinase—a type of chemical that destroys

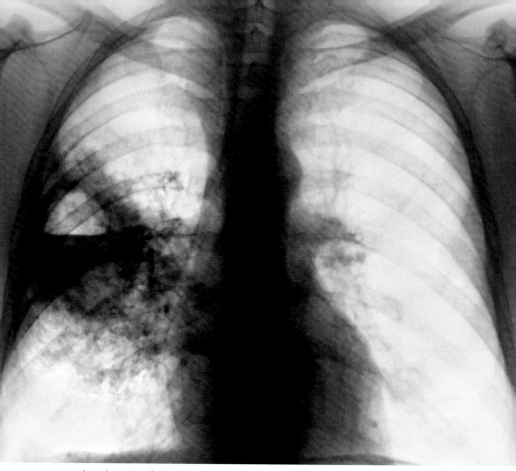

The damage from alpha-1 COPD is usually in the lower part of the lungs whereas most of the lung damage in people with non-alpha-1 COPD is in the upper lungs.

proteins. Alpha-1 antitrypsin is a proteinase inhibitor. When an individual has AAT deficiency, neutrolphil elastase is not neutralized. Thus, the enzyme keeps on working, and over time it builds up in the lungs and starts to destroy lung tissue, which is partly made of proteins. When this leads to COPD, many people refer to it as genetic COPD or alpha-1 COPD.

The lung damage in people with alpha-1 COPD differs from the damage in those with non-alpha-1 COPD. The damage in alpha-1 COPD is usually in the lower part of the lungs. Most of the lung damage in people with non-alpha-1 COPD is in the upper lungs.

Experts estimate that about one in twenty-five hundred Americans have AATD. It is one of the most common inherited

Alpha-1 Antitrypsin Deficiency

Parents can pass hereditary conditions to their offspring through their genes. Children receive genes from both parents. For each trait, a child receives one or more genes from the mother and corresponding genes from the father. Some diseases can result from a child's inheriting just one abnormal gene from one parent. Other diseases require abnormal genes from both parents. This is the case with alpha-1 antitrypsin deficiency. People with this disease inherit abnormal genes from both parents. Those who inherit one normal alpha-1 gene and one abnormal one do not have AATD. However, they are known as carriers because they can pass the defective gene to their offspring.

Many alpha-1 gene abnormalities can cause AATD disease. The most common abnormalities are known as S and Z. About one hundred thousand people in the United States have two Z alpha-1 genes and are said to have alpha-1 ZZ disease. Fewer people with AATD disease have alpha-1 SZ. Those with alpha-1 SZ have less chance of developing lung problems than those with alpha-1 ZZ do. People with two S gene mutations (alpha-1 SS) usually produce enough alpha-1 antitrypsin protein to protect the lungs from disease.

disorders among Caucasians. Individuals born with AAT gene mutations are extremely likely to develop COPD if they smoke or are otherwise exposed to lung irritants. However, even people who lack lung irritant exposure have an increased risk of developing COPD if they have AATD.

People with AATD tend to develop COPD earlier in life than others—often in their thirties and forties, compared to the sixties and seventies being the most common age for developing non-alpha-1 COPD. For this reason, lung specialists encourage people whose lifestyle puts them at risk for COPD to receive a genetic test for AATD. This is the only method of diagnosing AATD. That way, the individual can change behaviors such as smoking that increase the likelihood of developing COPD if he or she does have the gene mutation. "Early diagnosis can help an Alpha consider different lifestyles, professions or other personal decisions that could maintain or improve their health,"[27] states the Alpha-1 Foundation. Pulmonologists also recommend that everyone diagnosed with COPD undergo a blood test for the AATD mutation because the treatment for alpha-1 COPD differs slightly from that for other cases of COPD. Experts estimate that up to 3 percent of the people in the United States with COPD have undetected AATD.

Other Genetic Influences

Although alpha-1 deficiency is the best-understood genetic risk factor for COPD, researchers are also studying other genes that play a role. Researchers have determined that several genes on chromosome 15 in areas known as IREB2, HHIP, and FAM13A are associated with a genetic susceptibility to developing COPD, but no one has proved exactly which genes are involved. It can take many years to prove that certain genes cause or increase susceptibility to a particular disease. Scientists must painstakingly analyze the genomes (complete sets of DNA) from many people who have and do not have the disease to determine which genes are involved. Then they must experimentally show that the genes actually cause the disease.

Other researchers have come close to identifying genes on chromosome 19 that play a role in determining which smokers develop COPD. In February 2014 researchers at Weill Cornell Medical College reported that they discovered the first biological link between four abnormal genes on this chromosome and the lung damage associated with COPD. The gene abnormalities, coupled with smoking, lead to abnormal basal cells that line the airways. Basal cells are the first lung cells to show damage from smoking. Basal cells also contain stem cells (immature cells that can develop into specialized cells), and these stem cells produce three types of cells that protect, clean, and repopulate the airway lining. Researcher Ronald Crystal explains:

> Basal cells replace cells in that lining that are injured or that die, so without them, your lungs will become sick. . . . We believe that smoking reprograms basal cells, making some smokers with a certain genetic variant [mutation] more susceptible to COPD, but we don't know the details yet. . . . This is the first demonstration of COPD risk genes to an actual mechanism within cells that are critical for the maintenance of lung health. We doubt these four genes are

Sex and COPD

COPD used to affect men almost exclusively. However, today it affects men and women almost equally. The reasons for these changes vary in wealthy and impoverished nations. As the World Health Organization explains, "At one time, COPD was more common in men, but because of increased tobacco use among women in high-income countries, and the higher risk of exposure to indoor air pollution (such as solid fuel used for cooking and heating) in low-income countries, the disease now affects men and women almost equally."

Studies indicate that women who smoke are more susceptible to developing COPD than men who smoke are. Indeed, women who smoke are 37 percent more likely than men who smoke to develop COPD, even if these women start smoking later and smoke fewer cigarettes. Experts believe this may be due to differences in how men and women metabolize cigarette smoke.

Other research indicates that women who smoke are particularly vulnerable to developing the chronic bronchitis that goes along with COPD. In 2006, for example, 6.6 million women in the completely responsible for COPD. They are likely part of the story—we believe they play a central role in the very early events that lead to COPD, but they act within a very complex genetic-environment interaction.[28]

Lung Irritants

The environmental component of the gene-environment interactions that cause COPD consists of various types of lung irritants. Cigarette smoke is the most common lung irritant known to cause COPD in susceptible people. Indeed, studies show that up to 90 percent of COPD patients are current or former

United States were diagnosed with chronic bronchitis, compared to 2.9 million men. Men who smoke, on the other hand, are more likely to develop emphysema. In 2006 nearly 2.5 million men and 1.6 million women were diagnosed with emphysema.

World Health Organization. "Chronic Obstructive Pulmonary Disease," October 2013. www.who.int/mediacentre/factsheets/fs315/en.

Studies have indicated that women who smoke are more susceptible to developing COPD than are men who smoke.

cigarette smokers. Doctors find that the more cigarettes an individual smokes, the greater his or her chances are of developing COPD. Experts measure the amount someone has smoked in pack years. One pack year means that a smoker has smoked one pack of cigarettes (twenty cigarettes) per day for one year. One pack year totals about seventy-three hundred cigarettes. Someone who smokes two packs a day for one year would be assigned a smoking intensity score of two pack years. Any amount of smoking increases the risk of developing COPD, but experts find the risk is highest for people who smoke for twenty or more pack years.

Although cigarette smoke is the most common of the environmental irritants that cause COPD, it is not the only substance tied to the disease. Researchers have proved that smoking a pipe or cigars also increases the risk of COPD sub-

Research has shown that inhaling pipe or cigar smoke substantially increases the risk of COPD.

stantially. Many doctors believe that smoking marijuana does this as well, but studies have had contradictory results, so this issue is controversial. Pulmonologist Donald P. Tashkin of the University of California–Los Angeles, for example, has conducted research that he says indicates that regularly smoking marijuana does not impair lung function, and "no clear link to chronic obstructive pulmonary disease has been established."[29]

On the other hand, researchers Matthew G. Drake and Christopher G. Slatore of the Oregon Health and Science University believe that smoking marijuana may be even more likely to lead to COPD than is cigarette smoking. Drake and Slatore write, "Marijuana smoke contains many of the same harmful chemicals as tobacco smoke . . . marijuana users expose their lungs to a larger amount of smoke because they tend to inhale more deeply, smoke without filters, and hold their breath when they inhale."[30]

Secondhand smoke (being around people who smoke cigarettes or other substances) is another proven risk factor for COPD. Cigarette smoke contains more than seven thousand chemicals; some of the most toxic are arsenic, lead, carbon monoxide, hydrogen cyanide, and ammonia. The Canadian Lung Association explains:

> Two thirds of the smoke from a cigarette is not inhaled by the smoker, but enters the air around the smoker. Secondhand smoke has at least twice the amount of nicotine and tar as the smoke inhaled by the smoker. It has five times the amount of carbon monoxide, a deadly gas that robs the blood of oxygen. It also contains higher levels of ammonia (better known as window cleaner) and cadmium (also found in batteries). . . . Regular exposure to secondhand smoke increases the risk of lung disease by 25%.[31]

In addition, when a mother smokes during pregnancy, this raises the risk of COPD in her offspring because smoke impairs the development of the fetus's lungs. Researchers have also found that the mother's smoking causes fetal immune system damage, which can make the lungs especially prone to damage from inflammation.

Other Inhaled Substances

The various types of inhaled smoke are not the only substances that can lead to COPD. After long-term exposure to chemical fumes or dust in the workplace, 10 to 20 percent of people working in these conditions in the United States developed COPD. If individuals exposed to these workplace toxins also smoke, this enhances the adverse effects of the toxins and increases the risk of developing COPD even more.

Occupations associated with inhaled lung damage include coal mining, hard rock mining, digging tunnels, construction of all types, farming, and manufacturing plastics, clothing, rubber, leather, and food products. Transportation workers who work with aircraft, cars, buses, and trains are also often exposed to harmful by-products of burning fuel. People who live in places with a great deal of air pollution are also at increased risk for developing COPD. Doctors state that people with existing heart or lung diseases are especially susceptible to developing COPD after exposure to air pollution from fuel-burning vehicles.

Many homes, especially in developing countries, also contain large amounts of indoor air pollution that contribute to COPD. This comes from open fires or from burning coal or biomass for heating or in cookstoves. Biomass is biological material taken from living or recently living organisms. For instance, plant and animal waste products are often burned for fuel. According to the World Health Organization (WHO), "Around 3 billion people still cook and heat their homes using solid fuels in open fires and leaky stoves. About 2.7 billion burn biomass (wood, animal dung, crop waste) and a further 0.4 billion use coal. Most are poor, and live in developing countries."[32]

People exposed to these types of indoor pollution are two to three times more likely than normal to develop COPD. In fact, exposure to smoke from burning biomass accounts for about 50 percent of the cases of COPD diagnosed in developing countries. The disease results when small soot particles from smoke generated by burning these substances in poorly

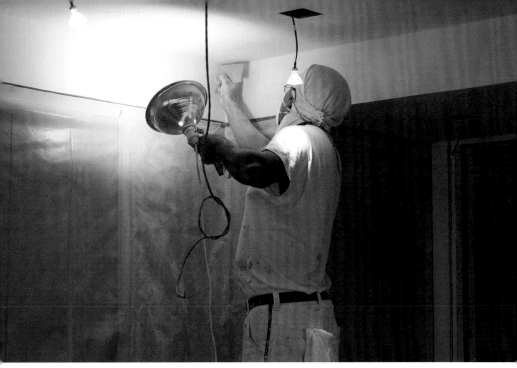

About 10 to 20 percent of people with COPD in the United States developed the disease after long-term exposure to chemical fumes or dust in the workplace.

ventilated rooms settles into and inflames the lungs. More than 1 million people die each year from COPD caused by this type of indoor pollution.

How Irritants Cause Lung Damage

Smoke and other lung irritants lead to various types of damage that can in turn lead to COPD in susceptible people. The damage is mostly caused by the inflammatory response of the immune system. White blood cells that rush to the lungs to attack the irritants release large quantities of cytokines such as leukotriene-4 and interleukin-8, which cause inflammation. These cells also release proteinases like elastase and cathepsin to destroy the foreign substances. At the same time, certain gene abnormalities can prevent the white blood cells from releasing antiproteinases to stop these proteinases from destroying lung tissue. One effect of long-term exposure to inflammation and proteinases is that these substances activate a chemical called epidermal growth factor receptor. Epidermal growth factor receptor makes mucus-producing glands in the bronchi increase in size and produce extra mucus in an attempt to protect lung tissue from the inflammation. Lung irritants like smoke also damage or destroy cilia in the airways. When cilia are not there to sweep away mucus, the mucus builds up and causes chronic bronchitis and airway obstructions. The chronic inflammation also leads lung cells to form scar tissue that can block the airways, and it damages or destroys alveoli so they cannot do their job.

In 2011 researchers at Johns Hopkins University discovered one factor that makes lung cells in people with COPD unable to withstand cell damage from inflammation. In response to substances that can damage cells, a protein called nuclear factor erythroid-2 (Nrf2) normally activates antioxidant chemicals in cells to protect them against damage. The researchers found that a type of white blood cells called macrophages show reduced Nrf2 activity in people with COPD. With insufficient Nrf2, antioxidants are not produced to fight damage to lung cells from irritants. In addition, the researchers found that insufficient Nrf2 activity after exposure to cigarette smoke renders macrophages unable to perform their usual job of engulfing and removing bacteria from lung cells. They believe this explains why people with COPD are especially vulnerable to developing lung infections.

Other studies have shown that ongoing exposure to lung irritants not only causes COPD, but also contributes to the exacerbations, or instances where symptoms worsen, that patients frequently experience. Many of these exacerbations occur when bacteria or viruses settle into damaged lungs and the immune system fails to kill these pathogens.

Other Contributing Factors

Researchers have determined that factors other than lung irritants also affect the risk of developing COPD. One factor that increases the risk is poverty. A 2014 report from the Global Initiative for Chronic Obstructive Lung Disease explains, "There is strong evidence that the risk of developing COPD is

Poverty contributes to mortality from COPD by adding unhealthful conditions to life, such as low birth weight, exposure to smoke and fumes from indoor cooking and heating devices (such as shown here), poor diet, and lack of medical care.

inversely related to socioeconomic status. It is not clear, however, whether this pattern reflects exposures to indoor and outdoor air pollutants, crowding, poor nutrition, infections, or other factors that are related to low socioeconomic status."[33]

A 2013 study by researchers at the National Heart and Lung Institute at Imperial College London shed some light on how poverty may influence COPD risk and the risk of dying from COPD. The study compared the effects of poverty and smoking on the incidence and mortality (death rate) associated with the disease. Results showed that many impoverished people die from COPD in areas where smoking is uncommon—in other words, people in England who die from COPD are more likely to be impoverished than to smoke. The researchers concluded that although poverty can affect the risk of getting COPD, its largest effects were on influencing whether someone dies from it. They believe poverty may affect the risk of death because of its association with low birth weight, exposure to indoor cookstoves and heating smoke, poor diet, and poor medical care.

Other research finds evidence that low birth weight and lungs that are not fully developed at birth occur most often in impoverished people. In turn, this can result from a mother's poor diet during pregnancy or from the mother's smoking. Several studies have found that babies with low birth weight are more likely to have reduced FEV1 values as adults. Such data led the authors of a 2011 study at the University of Padua in Italy to conclude, "Adult respiratory health is shaped early in life. . . . A combination of genetic and environmental factors in childhood may induce an 'early-life disadvantage' as influential as cigarette smoking for the risk of COPD in adulthood. . . . Individuals born with a low birth weight or small for gestational age are at higher risk of persistent airflow obstruction."[34]

How well the lungs develop during childhood and adolescence also affects COPD risk. Although the bronchial tube branches develop during the first trimester of pregnancy, the final development of alveoli does not occur until a child is about two years old. Then the lungs continue to grow and develop until the end of adolescence in women and into the mid-twenties in men. Anything that interferes with this growth and development, whether it is environmental irritants, lung infections, or asthma, raises the risk of COPD later in life. A 2010 study by a group of Norwegian researchers found that the effect of early life disadvantage factors "appears to persist.... In the struggle to prevent COPD, intervention in early life in addition to smoking prevention might help abate the growing COPD epidemic."[35] Indeed, although some effective treatments for COPD exist, experts have realized that the best way to deal with the widespread impact of the disease is to emphasize prevention so treatment is not necessary.

CHAPTER THREE

COPD Treatment

COPD treatment cannot cure the disease or reverse patients' lung damage, but it can help them live longer, fuller lives. Specialists emphasize that the most effective treatments involve a team of therapists who administer a customized treatment plan. Although each element of treatment is individualized for each patient, the goals of treatment are similar. Treatment aims to reduce symptoms and exacerbations, improve lung function, slow or halt disease progression, reduce the chances of dying from COPD, and improve overall quality of life.

The treatment team often includes a primary care doctor and/or pulmonologist, hospital doctors, respiratory therapists, nurses, dieticians, pharmacists, mental health therapists, and social workers. Not all patients require care by all these professionals, and individual needs may change during different phases of the disease.

The overall treatment program is referred to as pulmonary rehabilitation (PR). Some hospitals and clinics have special PR programs. Patients whose local medical centers do not have such programs often travel to those that do. After participating in these programs for several weeks, patients learn to continue on their own at home with assistance from local health care professionals. When exacerbations and worsening lung function occur, patients are usually treated in a hospital.

Smoking Cessation

Since smoking is the most common cause of COPD, a critical component of treatment involves smoking cessation for those who smoke. The Canadian Lung Association explains that quitting smoking is the best thing patients can do to feel better and limit lung damage: "By quitting smoking now, you can't undo the damage that's already been done, but you can protect your lungs from any more damage."[36]

However, since the nicotine in cigarettes is an addictive drug, it is very difficult for many people to quit. Like with other addictive drugs, patients who quit smoking experience cravings and withdrawal symptoms. These symptoms include headache, nausea, insomnia, and anxiety. One patient told COPD International that she smoked from the minute she woke up in the morning until going to bed at night. Doctors told her to stop when she was hospitalized three times with breathing difficulties, but she craved nicotine so much that she began smoking again each time she went home from the hospital. She finally realized she had to quit after she needed supplemental oxygen all the time. It took her four months,

Smoking withdrawal symptoms include headache, nausea, insomnia, and anxiety.

but once she quit she felt better and called quitting smoking "another chance at life."[37]

There are a variety of methods and programs to help smokers quit. Doctors find that smokers who use behavior therapy and nicotine replacement techniques have the best chances of permanently quitting. Behavior therapists help patients change their thinking and behavior so they can banish smoking from their lives. Therapists often recommend setting a firm "quit date," enlisting support from family and friends, and getting rid of all smoking supplies, including cigarettes and ashtrays.

Medications to Aid Smoking Cessation

Nicotine replacement therapy helps smokers change their behavior by giving them an alternative source of nicotine to satisfy their cravings while they are quitting. It can be administered in the form of patches, gum, nasal spray, inhalers, or lozenges. Doctors usually recommend continuing nicotine replacement therapy for ten to twelve weeks, but some patients need more or less time. Success rates vary for different treatment methods. For example, nicotine gum increases the chances of quitting by about 40 percent and nasal sprays by close to 100 percent.

Sometimes nicotine replacement therapy is combined with other antismoking drugs, or in some cases smokers use these other drugs without nicotine replacement. One such drug is bupropion (sold as Zyban or Wellbutrin). This is an antidepressant; its effects on smoking cessation are independent of its effects on depression. Bupropion contains no nicotine. It decreases nicotine cravings and withdrawal symptoms by blocking the stimulant effects of nicotine on the brain and increasing the amount of brain chemicals that activate the so-called reward centers in the brain. Studies show that bupropion is as effective as some forms of nicotine replacement therapy for some people.

Another drug approved for smoking cessation is varenicline (marketed as Chantix). This medication also blocks the effects

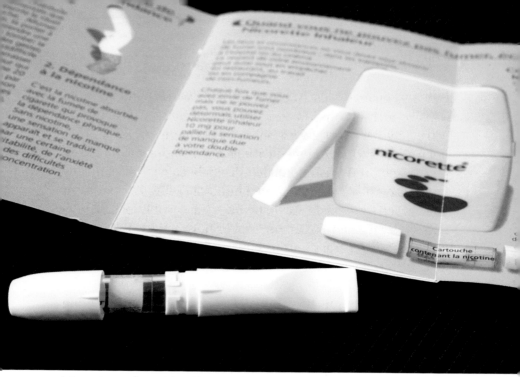

Nicotine replacement therapy helps smokers quit by giving them a smoke-free source of nicotine.

of nicotine on the brain. However, experts consider varenicline to be more effective than bupropion. When taken for twelve to twenty-four weeks, varenicline doubles, and in some cases triples, the chances of successfully quitting smoking.

Medications for COPD Control

Besides quitting smoking, most COPD patients benefit from medications that address COPD symptoms. The primary such medications are bronchodilators—drugs that dilate, or open up, the bronchial tubes. Some bronchodilators, known as controller medications, are used every day, even when a patient is breathing well. Others are used for quick relief of breathing problems and disease exacerbations.

Bronchodilators come in pill and inhaled forms. Patients usually require smaller doses of inhaled medications because they go directly into the lungs. However, proper technique is critical to ensure that the maximum amount of medicine is inhaled. Studies indicate that up to 50 percent of patients receive little or no benefit from their inhaled medications because of incorrect use. Elderly patients with cognitive problems or arthritis that makes holding an inhaler difficult are especially likely not to use inhalers correctly. In such cases doctors prescribe oral medications such as theophylline. But physicians prefer using inhaled drugs because "no clinically useful or effective oral bronchodilator without significant adverse effects exists for patients with chronic obstructive pulmonary disease (COPD),"[38] according to the book *ABC of COPD*. These adverse effects may include heart problems, headache, nausea and vomiting, abdominal pain, seizures, and insomnia.

Controller medications usually consist of long-acting bronchodilators that begin working in less than one hour and last from twelve to thirty-six hours. The most commonly used long-acting bronchodilators are long-acting beta2-agonists such as formoterol and anticholinergics such as tiotropium. Anticholinergics "are frequently preferred over beta-agonists for their minimal cardiac stimulatory effects and greater efficacy [effectiveness],"[39] according to a 2013 study reported in *Current Medicinal Chemistry*. However, long-acting beta2-agonists work better in patients with FEV1 greater than or equal to 50 percent of the predicted value, and some patients do best with combined beta2-agonists and anticholinergics.

How Controller Medicines Work

Both beta2-agonists and anticholinergics dilate the airways, but their mechanisms of action differ. Beta2-agonists work by stimulating adrenergic receptors (receptors on cells that take in the chemical adrenaline). Adrenaline stimulates the nervous system and loosens muscles throughout the body, including those in the heart. This raises the heart rate, which can be dangerous. The type of anticholinergics used to treat COPD, on the other hand, block muscarinic acetylcholine receptors in the airways. Acetylcholine is a neurotransmitter (brain chemical) that tightens muscles throughout the body. Muscarinic acetylcholine receptors are the specific type of acetylcholine receptors in airway muscle cells. Thus, anticholinergics that specifically block muscarinic acetylcholine receptors do not affect the heart or muscles other than those in the airways.

A new COPD controller drug called aclidinium bromide (brand name Tudorza Pressair), approved by the U.S. Food and Drug Administration in 2012, is even more likely than tiotropium to affect only airway muscarinic acetylcholine receptors. Thus, doctors believe it will prove to be even more effective in treating COPD without damaging the heart. Another advantage of

Types of Inhalers

COPD patients inhale most bronchodilators through the mouth using a handheld inhaler. Some patients have difficulties using some inhalers, so there are several kinds to choose from.

- The most common type is a pressurized metered dose inhaler (pMDI). These have a mouthpiece and a hand-controlled dispenser lever. Proper use involves exhaling, placing the mouthpiece between the lips, and pressing the dispenser while inhaling.

- Metered dose inhalers with a spacer are pMDIs with an attachment that automatically coordinates inhaling with dispensing the drug. The spacer holds the medicine after the patient pushes the dispenser and releases it when the person inhales.

- Dry powder inhalers use powdered rather than liquid drugs. The powder disintegrates into tiny particles that go into the lungs when the patient inhales from the inhaler. Some patients cannot use powder inhalers because they require a more forceful breath than other types of inhalers.

- Accuhalers and Turbohalers allow patients to inhale combinations of short- and long-acting bronchodilators.

aclidinium bromide is that the liver, which breaks down drugs, can rid the body of it more easily than it does other long-acting bronchodilators. This means that the drug is less likely to build up in the liver and damage it after long-term use.

Aclidinium acts within about thirty minutes of taking it and lasts for up to twenty-nine hours. Patients take it twice per day. Researchers who tested the drug in clinical trials concluded that "the twice-daily dosing regimen of aclidinium may also provide significant benefits at night and early morning when COPD symptoms are more burdensome."[40]

- Nebulizers create a mist of drug particles that are inhaled through a face mask or a mouthpiece. Nebulizers are easier for many patients to use than regular inhalers are.

- Some inhalers are designed to deliver particular drugs to the lungs. For example, HandiHalers are made for the drug tiotropium.

Several types of bronchodilator inhalers are marketed because some patients have difficulties using certain types.

Some doctors prescribe long-term use of inhaled corticosteroids such as beclomethasone dipropionate or fluticasone propionate along with beta agonists or anticholinergics. Corticosteroids reduce inflammation but also impair parts of the immune system that fight infections and cancers. They also have other adverse effects such as causing stomach ulcers, diabetes, thinning bones, depression, and weight gain, so their long-term use is very controversial. Some studies show that inhaled corticosteroids ease COPD patients' breathing and decrease disease exacerbations, but others show no positive effects. Doctors who prescribe these drugs use the lowest possible effective doses to minimize side effects.

Treatment for Exacerbations

One goal of treatment with long-acting controller medications is to decrease the number and intensity of exacerbations. The more exacerbations a patient has, the faster his or her lung function declines. However, patients can experience exacerbations even when their condition is stabilized with controller drugs. Exacerbations can range from mild to life-threatening and may include increased breathlessness and coughing, wheezing, chest tightness, weakness, confusion, lung infections, and an inability to breathe without a ventilator. Patients with serious exacerbations generally require care in a hospital.

Most exacerbations are treated with fast-acting bronchodilators, such as the anticholinergic antimuscarinic drug ipratropium bromide or the beta agonist salbutamol. Many of these drugs act in less than five minutes. Doctors say it is important for patients to use fast-acting bronchodilators as infrequently as possible, since frequent use is associated with heart disease, seizures, and other problems.

Many doctors also prescribe oral corticosteroids for exacerbations, since they are proven to improve COPD patients' lung function more quickly than fast-acting bronchodilators alone. As with inhaled corticosteroids used to control COPD, physicians prescribe the smallest effective dose and gradually reduce the dosage and discontinue the drugs as soon as possible to avoid dangerous side effects.

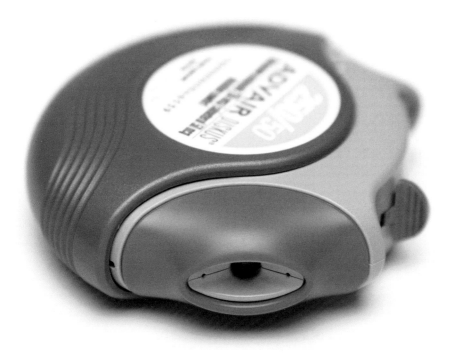

Fluticasone powder is administered through an inhalation device to help manage COPD.

Since many patients develop lung infections during exacerbations, treatment often involves using antibiotics to kill the bacteria that cause these infections as well. Some pulmonologists believe administering ongoing low doses of antibiotics reduces the number of exacerbations. However, this practice is controversial because it often makes bacteria resistant to these drugs and as a result makes the drugs less effective.

Treating Serious Exacerbations

Very serious exacerbations can include decreased blood oxygen levels and/or increased carbon dioxide levels that can lead to respiratory failure. COPD is in fact the most common cause of respiratory failure. Doctors perform blood tests for arterial blood gases (blood is taken from arteries, which contain oxygenated blood from the heart, rather than veins) to test for levels of oxygen and carbon dioxide that reveal respiratory failure. An alternative method of testing for blood oxygen levels is with a pulse oximeter clipped to a finger or ear lobe. Pulse oximeters measure oxygen saturation (the amount of oxygen in hemoglobin molecules in the blood) by determining how much light hemoglobin absorbs. Healthy adults usually have oxygen saturations of 95 to 98 percent at sea level.

There are two types of respiratory failure; each requires different treatments. Type 1 occurs when damaged alveoli prevent adequate amounts of oxygen from getting into the bloodstream. However, fewer functioning alveoli are needed to remove carbon dioxide from the blood, so people with type 1 respiratory failure still have normal carbon dioxide levels. Patients with type 1 respiratory failure have oxygen saturation levels of 88 percent or less. Doctors administer higher-than-normal oxygen concentrations until the patient's oxygen saturation level reaches 94 to 98 percent.

In type 2 respiratory failure, also known as hypercapnia, so many alveoli have been destroyed that the lungs cannot remove carbon dioxide from the blood. Thus, type 2 involves low oxygen and high carbon dioxide levels, which leads to respiratory acidosis without treatment. Respiratory acidosis causes internal organs to shut down and can be fatal. Patients with this type of respiratory failure need less-concentrated oxygen, with a goal of achieving 88 to 92 percent oxygen saturation. This is because balancing high carbon dioxide levels with higher oxygen saturations can exacerbate respiratory acidosis.

Breathing Therapy

Although some patients only need supplemental oxygen for exacerbations, many others benefit from using oxygen every day. Such patients carry portable oxygen tanks attached to nasal cannulae with them everywhere. According to a study reported in the journal *Chest*, "Oxygen was the first treatment shown to prolong life in people with COPD."[41] However, doctors stress the importance of using only the prescribed amount and concentration of oxygen. Many patients misunderstand

Many COPD patients increase their oxygen intake by using a portable oxygen tank hooked up to a nasal or throat cannula.

the reasons for needing oxygen and end up taking either too much or too little. Both extremes can be dangerous. Too little oxygen can deprive the brain, heart, and other organs of the oxygen they need to function. Too much oxygen tells the brain to slow the rate of inhaling and exhaling. The lack of exhalations can result in carbon dioxide building up in the blood.

The American Thoracic Society explains that patients only need supplemental oxygen when their blood oxygen levels are too low: "Oxygen is probably one of the least understood and misused therapies for people with COPD. . . . Breathlessness is not a reliable way of determining if you need oxygen. Sometimes, you can be very short of breath and not need oxygen; other times your breathing may feel okay, but you are not getting enough oxygen. Oxygen is not given to treat breathlessness."[42]

Although some people use oxygen all the time, some only need short bursts of oxygen after exercise, and others only need oxygen while they sleep. This is because everyone's breathing is shallower during sleep, and blood oxygen levels normally drop somewhat. Still other patients only require supplemental oxygen when they travel by airplane. This is because the cabin pressure in airplanes is kept at the equivalent of 8,000 feet (2,438m) above ground. The air at higher altitudes contains less oxygen than at sea level; this is why it is harder to breathe at high elevations. Oxygen saturation levels can fall during air travel, and such a drop can lead to severe breathlessness in people with COPD unless they use supplemental oxygen.

Besides using supplemental oxygen, other types of breathing assists can help COPD patients in their everyday lives. Those with trapped mucus often use airway clearance devices to loosen this mucus. Some devices are small, tube-like contraptions with valves or other vibrating parts. Some consist of vests that vibrate against the chest.

Many patients use continuous positive airway pressure (CPAP) or bilevel positive airway pressure (BiPAP) machines to help them breathe when asleep or as needed when awake, either at home or in a hospital. CPAP machines force air through the lungs to keep the airways open. They are connected to a face mask with a hose. BiPAPs reverse the air pressure to help patients exhale, in addition to applying pressure to help with inhalation. BiPAP and CPAP are called noninvasive ventilators since they use a face mask rather than placing a breathing tube down a patient's throat. They are also called assistive devices because they assist the patient with breathing rather than taking over the breathing process. Invasive ventilators, on the other hand, breathe for patients who cannot breathe on their own and are used in hospital intensive care units.

Pulmonary Rehabilitation

Medical doctors prescribe the oxygen therapy and medication portions of a total PR program. However, COPD experts emphasize that the other aspects of these programs, such as exercise, are equally important for allowing patients to feel and function as well as possible. As the NHLBI explains, "PR doesn't replace medical therapy. Instead, it's used with medical therapy and may include exercise training, nutritional counseling, education on your lung disease . . . energy conserving techniques, breathing strategies, psychological counseling and/or support group."[43] PR can be administered at outpatient clinics or in a patient's home, depending on individual needs.

COPD experts say regular exercise is an extremely important part of PR, unless patients suffer from certain types of heart disease. Therapists find, however, that many patients believe they cannot or should not exercise because they become short of breath. The American Thoracic Society explains that although dyspnea is uncomfortable, "it does not mean that the person is further damaging their lungs by doing things that make them breathless. Unfortunately, people try to avoid this feeling by doing fewer activities or activities less often . . . avoiding activities leads to getting out of shape or becoming deconditioned. Becoming deconditioned can result in even more shortness of breath with activity."[44] The therapists who run PR programs teach patients how to gradually build up their strength with moderate exercises such as walking and strength training with light weights. Most therapists recommend that patients exercise for about thirty minutes at least three times per week.

Another important part of PR involves teaching patients breathing and airway clearance techniques. Respiratory therapists are usually the PR team members who administer these treatments. One such technique is pursed lip breathing. Here, the patient pushes his or her lips together when exhaling. This creates pressure that slows the flow of air out of the lungs and helps keep the airways open. Another technique called slow, deep breathing helps patients breathe more easily while exercising and also helps them avoid rapid, shallow breathing at other times. Other techniques include energy conservation, which teaches patients how to position the head and body to use the least amount of energy, allowing patients to save their energy for necessary tasks.

Diet and COPD

Another important part of PR is diet. Many people with COPD are underweight and malnourished because working hard to breathe often means they need extra calories to stay alive. Other patients are overweight because they do not exercise. Nutritionists on the PR team therefore prescribe nutritious, balanced meals to help patients achieve a healthy weight and adequate nutrition.

One measure that can help reduce obesity is eating smaller, more frequent meals. This can also help patients breathe more easily, since having a full stomach can push against the lungs and worsen breathing difficulties. Nutritionists also recom-

Broccoli contains an antioxidant similar to the chemical sulforaphane, which researchers have discovered specifically reduces lung inflammation in mice and humans with COPD.

mend that patients eat a diet high in fiber and whole grains and low in salt. This has been proven to improve lung function in many patients by preventing the water retention that can impair breathing. Other studies indicate that nitrites found in cured meats such as hot dogs can worsen breathing, so patients are urged to avoid these substances.

A study reported in 2014 by researchers at the University of Nebraska Medical Center confirmed that diet is indeed important in COPD treatment. This study found that COPD patients who eat fruit, fish, and dairy products have better lung function and fewer symptoms than those who do not. Lead researcher Corrine Hanson states, "I think the take-away is that diet may be a modifiable factor for COPD patients. When we think about diet and disease, we usually think about heart disease and diabetes. But people with lung disease should be thinking about diet too."[45]

Researchers at Johns Hopkins University found that eating broccoli may be especially beneficial for COPD patients. Broccoli contains an antioxidant similar to the chemical sulforaphane, which the researchers discovered specifically reduces lung inflammation in mice and humans with COPD. Sulforaphane does this by increasing Nrf2 levels in lung cells. The researchers found that sulforaphane also enhances the ability of macrophages taken from COPD patients' lungs to engulf and remove bacteria in laboratory cultures. They are conducting further research to determine whether eating broccoli and/or taking sulforaphane supplements leads to improvements in COPD symptoms.

Surgery for COPD

When PR and other standard COPD treatments do not work, doctors sometimes perform surgery to help improve lung function. However, since COPD patients are three to five times more likely than normal to experience surgical complications, surgery is only considered in dire cases. One of the most common surgeries is known as bullectomy. It involves removing bullae (air-filled blisters in the lungs of people with emphysema) and can help people with advanced emphysema breathe more easily. Another surgery is lung volume reduction surgery. Here, surgeons remove entire lung areas that have poorly functioning cells. This often helps areas with healthier cells operate more efficiently.

Another surgery, lung transplantation, is used as a last resort in patients with major breathing problems who do not respond to other treatments and who have quit smoking. Surgeons transplant lungs from deceased donors into transplant recipients. The operation is risky and requires recipients to take immunosuppressive drugs for the rest of their lives to keep them from rejecting the donated lungs. These drugs can threaten overall immune system strength. But many recipients like John Oberton say the procedure is worthwhile. Oberton states in a 2014 Temple University news article that he "feels reborn—like I have a second chance at life."[46] Before his transplant, Oberton could barely breathe and needed a wheelchair to get around. Afterward, he could lead an active life and could even help neighbors shovel snow off their driveways.

Alternative Treatments

Although treatments like lung transplants and PR can make life better for people with COPD, the fact that there is no cure or method of reversing lung damage leads some patients to seek alternative treatments outside mainstream medicine. Some of these treatments involve taking vitamins or herbs. The U.S. Food and Drug Administration points out that these supplements are not subject to rigorous testing like drugs are in the United States, and manufacturers often make exaggerated claims about their effectiveness. Some patients find supplements to be helpful, but others find them ineffective or harmful. This is why experts like those at the University of Maryland Medical Center advise patients to speak with a physician before trying supplements, especially since "supplements may have side effects or interact with medications."[47]

In other cases patients travel to countries like Russia or Mexico that allow unproven stem cell or other types of cell injections advertised as miracle cures to be performed. One doctor in Mexico named Luis Velazquez, for example, advertises "live cell therapy" in which he injects patients with lung cells taken from sharks. He claims this regenerates lung tissue and cures a

Alpha-1 Treatment

People with alpha-1 COPD receive the same types of treatment as other COPD patients, but there is an additional therapy called augmentation therapy available to them. Here, doctors infuse alpha-1 antitrypsin protein into the bloodstream through an intravenous line. Drug manufacturers make the infusion product by purifying supplies of the protein obtained from healthy donors' plasma (the liquid part of blood). The procedure augments (increases) the amount of this protein in the body. Since a lack of alpha-1 antitrypsin protein is responsible for the lung damage in patients with AATD, augmentation therapy can slow or stop the progression of this type of COPD. A study reported in 2013 by researchers at the University Health Network in Toronto, Canada, found that the augmentation product Zemaira significantly slowed the progression of emphysema in patients with alpha-1 COPD. The therapy did not, however, reverse lung damage, nor is it a cure.

Patients usually receive augmentation therapy once per week. Most patients tolerate the medication well, though some experience headaches, muscle and joint pain, and other flu-like symptoms. People with heart disease may also experience increased shortness of breath. There are four augmentation products approved for use in the United States: Prolastin-C®, Aralast NP™, Zemaira®, and Glassia®.

variety of ailments. Although legitimate doctors are testing stem cell treatments for this purpose, thus far, none have proven to be safe and effective for treating COPD. As the book *Understanding and Living with COPD* states, "There is absolutely no evidence that any clinic outside of the United States has surpassed what has been discovered and accomplished to date by all the legitimate stem cell researchers in the world."[48] Thus, COPD remains a treatable but not yet curable chronic disease.

CHAPTER FOUR

Living with COPD

Living with an incurable chronic disease like COPD can be emotionally and physically challenging. Many patients experience panic, anxiety, depression, and a variety of other intense emotions from the moment of diagnosis onward. These emotional reactions can have a profound effect on patients' quality of life and treatment compliance and can even affect disease progression. In fact, states the book *ABC of COPD*, "anxiety and depression often coexist in patients with COPD and are under-recognised and undertreated. . . . [They] may be associated with poorer quality of life, reduced survival, persistent smoking, higher hospital admission rate and more symptoms."[49]

Studies on depression indicate that several factors influence the relationship between COPD and depression. One such factor is that some treatment medications, such as corticosteroids, can cause or worsen existing depression. Another factor is the severity of an individual's disease. Researchers have found that anywhere from 40 to 70 percent of people with severe COPD are depressed, and about 20 percent with mild COPD are depressed. However, in some cases worsening disease leads to depression, but in others the opposite is true. In cases where depression precedes worsening COPD, studies indicate that this often happens because depression makes patients less likely to give up smoking or follow other parts of a treatment plan, so COPD worsens faster. Being depressed also influences the probability that a patient will be admitted to a hospital after being seen for a COPD exacerbation in an emergency room. COPD patients who are depressed or anxious are admitted to the hospital 52 percent more often compared to 19 percent of those who are not depressed or anxious.

The COPD Diagnosis

For many patients depression or other feelings of being overwhelmed stem from the shock of their diagnosis. Whereas some patients, especially smokers, are not surprised by their diagnosis, others are very surprised and find the shock overwhelming. A longtime smoker named Susie Bowers, for example, describes

Studies indicate a relationship between COPD and depression. Some COPD medications can cause or worsen existing depression.

her reaction when her physician diagnosed her with COPD and ordered oxygen to be delivered to her home:

> Oxygen! I thought. No, he can't be serious. Too stunned to ask questions, I nodded as he referred me to a pulmonary specialist. . . . That day changed my life forever. In the blink of an eye, I went from an independent, energetic newspaper editor with a bright future to a disabled, chronically ill patient who had to rely on oxygen at night and medications by day to breathe more easily.[50]

For Jean McCathern, the shock of being diagnosed with alpha-1 COPD at age forty-eight was magnified by twenty-four frustrating years of being misdiagnosed with asthma and al-

The progressive nature of COPD causes the patient's coping challenges to also progressively intensify as his or her physical condition worsens.

lergies. Despite steadily worsening lung function that forced McCathern to quit her job in the air force, doctors did not think to test her for alpha-1 deficiency when the treatments they prescribed for asthma and allergies were ineffective. Mc-Cathern told the *Washington Post* that she followed doctors' orders to give away her beloved cat, stop attending the hockey games she enjoyed watching (because being in crowded places increased her risk of lung infections), and not pursue other favorite activities because her doctors believed these factors worsened her asthma. These sacrifices and the knowledge that her misdiagnosis allowed COPD to progress to the point that she needed a lung transplant made the eventual diagnosis "a pretty big shock. . . . Everything stopped,"[51] she stated.

Many people with COPD find the diagnosis to be traumatic, but others find it even more difficult to deal with once their condition worsens. A patient named Vera Franks, for example, writes on the Emphysema Foundation for Our Right to Survive website that the full emotional impact of COPD did not affect her until she needed oxygen all the time: "Being told you have COPD is hard enough, accepting the fact you are forever attached to a hose to just simply live is not easy."[52] For others, the progressive nature of COPD causes the coping challenges to progressively intensify as their physical condition worsens. As COPD patient and author R.D. Martin explains in his book *Understanding and Living with COPD*, "As soon as we adjust to our current abilities (or is that disabilities?), those abilities become even less, and we start once again readjusting."[53]

Factors That Trigger Coping Challenges

Different patients find different aspects of living with COPD to be the most difficult to cope with and, in some people, the most likely to trigger depression. For instance, although Bowers was shocked by her diagnosis, she did not become deeply depressed until she had to stop working. She writes that her depression stemmed from her perception that "I had become my illness. I had no life of my own—merely a life of survival."[54] Without her job, Bowers felt like she lost her reason for living.

For some patients feelings of loss or depression stem primarily from the shame and guilt they feel about their smoking causing COPD and shortening their life span. A 2010 study by Swedish researchers found that patients who suffer from guilt and shame often feel worthless because they cannot work or complete ordinary tasks, but at the same time they believe they have no right to complain because the disease is their fault. When families and friends seem unsympathetic and resent helping out as well, this often makes patients feel isolated and even more unworthy of leading a fulfilling, joyful life. One patient who participated in the study told the researchers that guilt, shame, and an inability to function well made her feel like life was futile: "Well, you feel a bit like—to put it in a nutshell—that it is rather pointless continuing."[55]

Indeed, feelings of futility that come from the lifestyle and relationship changes COPD imposes are among the most stressful aspect of living with the disease for many people. A study by researchers at the University of Adelaide in Australia indicates that COPD exerts this type of influence through a combination of physical and emotional factors, including "restriction of activities, interference with sleep, and limitations of social life. . . . It is not surprising that COPD significantly affects the sufferer's mental health."[56]

Dealing with Coping Challenges

Pulmonologists and others who care for COPD patients are beginning to realize that regularly evaluating patients' mental state is an important part of treatment because depressed, anxious people are less likely to comply with treatment plans. Thus, mental health professionals are playing an increasing role in PR. Studies show that patients who are depressed benefit most from antidepressant medications combined with psychotherapy. Many types of psychotherapy can help, but cognitive behavioral therapies are among the most successful. Here, therapists help patients change their ways of thinking and behaving so they feel empowered to do whatever is necessary to live as fully as possible within the constraints imposed by COPD. For example, many patients find that changing thought

Persistence Pays Off

One of Steve Wolbrink's favorite pastimes was flying private planes. But after he was diagnosed with COPD, the Federal Aviation Administration (FAA) refused to renew his pilot's license because he failed to meet the lung function requirements. Wolbrink petitioned the FAA to reconsider his application, but it refused. Unwilling to give up, Wolbrink enlisted the help of U.S. senator Tom Daschle from his home state of South Dakota. Daschle wrote the FAA a letter, and the FAA finally agreed to consider Wolbrink's pilot's license application if he underwent blood oxygen tests in an altitude chamber. An altitude chamber is a machine that mimics the effects of flying at different altitudes.

Physician Warren Jensen conducted Wolbrink's oxygen tests and found that Wolbrink could fly safely at most altitudes. The FAA granted him a license with the restriction that he regularly monitor his blood oxygen levels during flights and that he carry an oxygen tank in case he needs supplemental oxygen. Thus, Wolbrink's perseverance allowed him to continue his hobby. An added bonus to his efforts was that Wolbrink now helps Jensen teach students at the University of North Dakota about COPD.

patterns that say "poor me" to those that say "I'm grateful for the blessings in my life" is a powerful method of lessening depression and other negative mental states. Therapists also employ cognitive behavioral techniques with patients who are not depressed but are having other types of coping difficulties, such as adjusting to smoking cessation, feeling overwhelmed by the need to take daily medications, or feeling isolated by a lack of family and social support.

Other measures that help patients cope are educating oneself about the disease and joining support groups consisting of other patients. These measures help promote a sense of empowerment that often leads to behavior changes that in

Cognitive-behavioral therapy (CBT) has proved successful in many cases of coping with COPD. CBT helps patients change their ways of thinking and behaving so they feel more empowered to do whatever is necessary to live as fully as possible within the constraints imposed by COPD.

turn enhance a healthy mental state. Education and support groups are also likely to reduce patients' depression and anxiety because feelings of empowerment diminish the sense of helplessness that goes along with these conditions. In addition, these resources diminish the feelings of isolation many patients experience. Many patients report that receiving and giving emotional and practical support in support groups and similar communities gives them a renewed sense of hope and purpose.

Indeed, the main reason Martin wrote *Understanding and Living with COPD* was to offer a source of understanding and support to his fellow COPD sufferers. In one section of the book, he reveals that a critical catalyst for helping him overcome negative, self-defeating thoughts and behaviors was forgiving himself for smoking and causing his disease. Once he forgave himself, he was able to focus on leading the best life possible. Thus, he encourages people struggling with feelings of isolation and guilt over causing their disease to learn to forgive themselves. "You can forgive yourself in the same manner you forgive others for their imperfections or past actions,"[57] he writes.

Support Groups and Advocacy

Many patients find that they benefit from learning about how others, like Martin, overcome various hurdles to live satisfying lives with COPD. Often, this knowledge inspires the courage and know-how that helps other individuals make similar changes. One alpha-1 COPD patient named Roger Bray became widely known in the COPD community for inspiring others to turn their lives around. Bray did not want to stop leading an active life after his diagnosis, so he developed a life plan he calls his "just out of reach"[58] philosophy. He broke his goals into small steps to allow himself to achieve a series of milestones that were just beyond his reach. One goal was to jog around the track at a neighborhood park. Bray started by slowly walking around the track and gradually advanced to slowly jogging short distances. Finally, he was able to jog around the entire track. Bray began sharing his technique with others in his support group, and many applied the technique to improve their own lives with COPD.

Many other COPD patients who have overcome obstacles make it their life's mission to help educate the public and advocate for COPD research, along with supporting fellow patients through support groups. Bunny Music, for example, nearly died from COPD, until she finally found the strength to quit smoking. She became an outspoken antismoking advocate who often speaks to other COPD patients and the public in hopes of motivating more people to quit. "I try to show people what they're headed for when they continue to smoke. Most of the time it falls on deaf ears. But there have been times that I've gotten through, and that makes me very glad,"[59] she writes on the COPD International website.

Sue Binnal of Massachusetts had to retire from her job because of alpha-1 COPD but found that she also derived satisfaction from becoming active in local and national alpha-1 support and advocacy groups. She speaks with other patients on a COPD information line, lobbies lawmakers on behalf of COPD researchers, and helps organize the annual Escape to the Cape Bike Trek in her area that raises money for research and awareness of alpha-1 COPD. In 2006 Binnal suffered a heart attack and was unable to participate in the event but still insisted on coordinating it from her hospital bed. The following year she again coordinated the trek and rode her bicycle 14 miles (22.5km) as a participant.

Many patients find that they benefit from learning about how others have overcome various hurdles to live satisfying lives with COPD.

Daily Life with COPD

Although many patients forge ahead to live active, engaged lives, physicians emphasize that it is still important for them to understand that COPD makes certain lifestyle changes necessary. For instance, since patients are very susceptible to lung infections, doctors recommend that they wash their hands frequently, not share towels or eating utensils, and wipe surfaces that other people touch, such as doorknobs, shopping carts, and menus, with disinfecting wipes. They also recommend wearing a mask in public or avoiding people who are sick. Some patients say others have accused them of being rude when they do things like leaving a room if it contains someone who is sneezing, but experts say it is more important to avoid exacerbations and infections than to worry about being called rude. As Martin explains, "Choose your events carefully, and don't let family or friends dictate what is safe for you. It is your responsibility [even though] you might lose friends along the way and people might give up on inviting you."[60]

Another important measure patients can take to live as well as possible is paying attention to which factors affect breathing capacity. For instance, substances like perfumes, cigarette smoke, pesticides, and cleaning supplies trigger breathing difficulties in many people with COPD. Patients can avoid situations in which these substances are present, even if it means asking visitors to one's home to avoid smoking or wearing perfume or asking relatives to refrain from using products with bleach when the person with COPD is present. Many patients also install air filters in their homes to trap particles that can irritate the lungs.

Despite their best efforts, however, most COPD patients encounter medical emergencies, and experts say it is important always to be prepared. Most patients wear medical alert bracelets or necklaces or carry a flash drive containing their medical information on a keychain. This way, paramedics called to the scene can quickly identify their medical condition and start appropriate treatment when an emergency occurs. Many patients also keep a small suitcase packed so they are ready to go to a hospital at a moment's notice if a breathing emergency occurs.

Many COPD patients consider the everyday issues they face to be challenging enough, but others who wish to add travel to their lives must be willing to preplan and deal with the special arrangements required in order to make travel possible. Whether they travel by car, train, plane, or ship, arrangements must be made to have oxygen tanks refilled during travel and once they reach a destination. Different airlines, cruise ships, and train operators have different policies on oxygen tanks. Some do not allow them on board, but others are willing to help patients arrange for oxygen suppliers to get through security checkpoints to refill the person's tanks. Most patients who make the effort to attend to all these details say it is well worth it since travel experiences enhance their quality of life.

Effects on Families

Besides affecting every aspect of patients' lives, COPD also has profound effects on their families. This is especially true when the patient is severely ill, has frequent exacerbations, or when family members must care for the patient at home. The role of a spouse may become that of a caretaker. If a patient is unmarried, other relatives may have to step in for caregiving unless the family can afford a paid caregiver or the patient goes to live in a nursing home. Federal laws such as the Family and Medical Leave Act mandate that people cannot be fired for taking up to twelve weeks of unpaid leave per year to attend to a family member's medical needs. However, many spouses or other relatives cannot afford to stop working temporarily or permanently to care for a sick individual. Being faced with this type of situation can lead to resentment and stress for the patient and family members involved.

For other families, the fact that many COPD patients must stop working imposes significant challenges. The Americans with Disabilities Act prevents employers from firing those with

Cannula Versus Trans-Trache

For many patients who need oxygen, one of the most difficult parts of living with COPD is wearing the nose cannula that delivers the oxygen. Having people stare at their cannula or enduring comments about smokers deserving lung disease motivates many patients to remain isolated in their homes. However, there is an alternative called a Trans-Trache that many patients say dramatically improves their willingness to venture out with oxygen. In addition, many find that the Trans-Trache improves their health. The Trans-Trache is a portable invasive ventilation system—that is, it involves a doctor making a hole in the neck and inserting flexible plastic tubing that hooks up to an oxygen hose attached to an oxygen tank. A patient named Kathie told COPD International that even though the Trans-Trache tubing must be cleaned daily, switching to it was worthwhile. Her oxygen saturation levels improved, and she says, "My brain feels clearer and I no longer feel handicapped because of that nasal cannula hanging on my face. My O_2 [oxygen] tank is carried in a shoulder bag and the tubing is under the clothing. I sometimes wear a scarf to cover the TransTrache but even without covering, it is a lot less visible than that nose hose. Most people look at your face, not your throat."

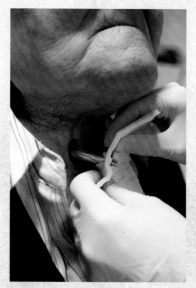

Kathie. "TransTrache: A Personal Experience." COPD International. www.copd-international.com/library/transtrache.htm.

A plastic tube is inserted into an opening in a COPD patient's throat as part of a Trans-Trache procedure.

disabilities like COPD as long as they are able to perform their jobs with reasonable accommodations. An example of a reasonable accommodation would be requesting a two-hour lunch break once a week to go for respiratory therapy and making up the time on another day. An unreasonable accommodation might be asking an employer to spend thousands of dollars installing an elevator for the COPD patient's use. But even with this law, many patients become unable to work at all as their disease progresses. This can result in financial difficulties for the family. Some patients are eligible for Social Security disability, but it is rarely enough to live on.

For Don Davis and his wife, the most stressful part of his diagnosis at age forty with alpha-1 COPD was uncertainty over how long he would be able to support and care for his family. As Davis told the Alpha-1 Foundation, "We had three young kids and we really had no idea what this meant for our future. One doctor told me I might only have three years to live."[61]

Some families are forced to make a variety of drastic changes to accommodate the family member with COPD. For example, Lisa Kosak and her family lived at an altitude of 7,000 feet (2,134m) in the mountains in Colorado when she was diagnosed with COPD. She required supplemental oxygen all the time, and her doctors recommended that she and her family move to a lower altitude to make it easier for her to breathe. They moved to Florida, and her need for oxygen disappeared.

Planning Ahead

Numerous COPD patients and families say that one of the most unpleasant, but necessary, aspects of living with the disease is facing the fact that COPD is fatal and will probably shorten the patient's life to some degree. Along with this realization comes the unpleasant task of the patient's speaking with family members about his or her wishes for end-of-life care. Most people do not wish to be kept alive by machines when they reach the point of being completely unable to breathe on their own and have no hope of getting better. In addition to verbally expressing such wishes to the family, legal experts say it is critical for

In addition to signing a traditional will that distributes one's property after death, many people also sign a living will, which indicates an individual's wishes for medical care in the event he or she is alive but unable to communicate.

patients to sign legal documents that spell out these wishes and specify who is authorized to make decisions if the patient is in a coma or otherwise incapacitated. Many people sign a living will for this purpose, in addition to signing a traditional will that distributes one's property after death. Living wills specify an individual's wishes for medical care while he or she is alive but unable to communicate.

Speaking about these matters is difficult for anyone, and many families tend to put off doing so. However, legal expert Martin M. Shenkman points out in his book *Estate and Financial Planning for People Living with COPD*, "The more openly you discuss your feelings with family, friends, and loved ones, the more likely that you can ease the burden of the decision making they face."[62]

Whatever the challenges for COPD patients and families may be, doctors find that those who accept and deal with the limitations the disease imposes and forge ahead lead the most satisfying lives and cope best with setbacks, no matter how severe they may be. As COPD patient Michelle Wisniewski states in an article on the Alpha-1 Foundation website, "You take what's there and you enjoy it; you can make anything you want out of your life."[63]

CHAPTER FIVE

The Future

Although modern treatments and patient support are helping many COPD patients live longer and more productive lives, the prevalence and personal, social, and economic burdens the disease imposes continue to grow as the population ages and more and more people are diagnosed after years of worsening lung damage. A 2014 study by the Centers for Disease Control and Prevention estimates that the costs associated with COPD will increase from $32.1 billion in 2010 to $49 billion by 2020 in the United States. However, COPD experts and advocacy groups believe that increased research and awareness campaigns can help limit these monetary increases, along with diminishing the emotional and physical toll COPD takes on patients and families.

For many years governments and medical researchers paid little attention to COPD, but that is starting to change. In August 2013, for the first time, WHO listed COPD as a priority disease that needs more attention and funding for research and treatment. At the same time, numerous governments realized the importance of investing in research and awareness campaigns. In May 2013, for instance, representatives from numerous American health agencies met to discuss ways to enhance COPD research and awareness. COPD experts and people affected by the disease hope that these events, along with ongoing and new research into COPD diagnosis, causes, treatment, and prevention, will help reduce the personal and societal impact of COPD in the future.

COPD Costs

Costs attributable to having COPD were $32.1 billion in 2010 with a projected increase to $49.0 billion by 2020.

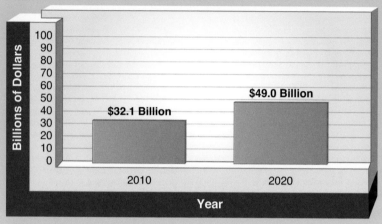

Medicare paid 51% of those costs with 25% paid by Medicaid and 18% by private insurance in 2010.

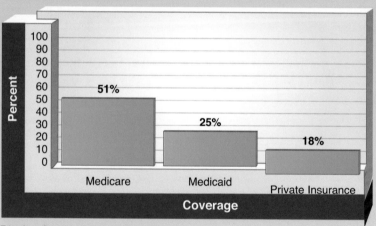

Taken from: Centers for Disease Control and Prevention.

Awareness Campaigns

Several programs backed by the American College of Chest Physicians, the American Lung Association, and other physician and patient advocacy organizations target physicians, patients, and the public to increase awareness of all aspects of COPD. One program directed at primary care physicians grew out of a 2007 study called the Primary Care Physician Needs Assessment. The COPD Foundation and an organization called Outcomes Inc. conducted this study to determine which areas of COPD care by primary care doctors needed improvement. The study found that 61.1 percent of primary care physicians in the United States did not think they received adequate education about COPD. Another 35.2 percent did not know how to use spirometry to diagnose COPD, and only 36 percent prescribed long-acting bronchodilators, which pulmonologists consider to be the best medications for controlling COPD in most patients. As a result of this study, the COPD Foundation put together an extensive physician education program. A recent article on the foundation's website states, "Continuing Medical Education (CME) events and workshops have proven

A COPD patient consults with a doctor about treatment. A study found that 61.1 percent of primary care physicians in the United States do not think they have received adequate education about COPD.

to be successful in spreading awareness of best practices in COPD diagnosis and management."[64] Despite these successes, the foundation points out that many primary care physicians are still unaware of how to care for people with COPD, so educational efforts are ongoing.

Other programs, such as NHLBI's Learn More Breathe Better® campaign, seek to enhance public awareness of the disease. Learn More Breathe Better® is mainly directed at people over age forty-five, especially those who smoke or used to smoke. The program uses public service announcements, social media, videos, newsletters, and community outreach to educate people about COPD symptoms, diagnosis, prevention, and treatment. NHLBI also works with COPD and lung foundations to sponsor National COPD Awareness Day each November. Another annual event, World COPD Day, is sponsored by the Global Initiative for Chronic Obstructive Lung Disease.

COPD Prevention

Along with COPD awareness programs have emerged numerous worldwide COPD prevention campaigns. Prevention campaigns work hand-in-hand with antismoking and anti–air pollution programs to promote laws that prohibit smoking in public and that regulate other sources of pollution. WHO is one organization committed to international efforts to reduce smoking. Its Framework Convention on Tobacco Control and its Global Alliance Against Chronic Respiratory Diseases actively promote antismoking measures. In discussing the importance of these efforts, WHO pointed out in 2013 that "total deaths from COPD are projected to increase by more than 30 percent in the next 10 years without interventions to cut risks, especially exposure to tobacco smoke."[65]

Since indoor pollution from burning biomass or coal leads to more than 1 million deaths from COPD per year in developing countries, WHO and other organizations like the Global Alliance for Clean Cookstoves are also leading efforts to promote new cookstove designs that reduce indoor pollution. The WHO website explains what the organization is doing to address this

COPD prevention campaigns work hand-in-hand with antismoking and other clean-air programs to promote laws that prohibit smoking in public and regulate other sources of pollution.

issue: "WHO is leading efforts to evaluate which of these new technologies produce the least emissions and thus are most optimal for health. WHO is also providing technical support to countries in their own evaluations and scale up of healthy-promoting stove technologies . . . [and] preparing new indoor air quality guidelines."[66]

Research into Causes

COPD experts believe that these types of prevention efforts will benefit from increased knowledge about how factors such as smoke cause the disease, so numerous studies relating to causes are under way. Better understanding of causes can improve diagnostic and treatment strategies as well. One question that has emerged as more and more women are developing COPD is why females are more susceptible to the disease than males are. Several recent studies indicate that the female hormone estrogen makes women more susceptible to lung damage if they smoke. Doctors believe this may be partly because estrogen breaks down the nicotine in cigarette smoke faster than the lungs can expel it. In addition, scientists believe that since females' airways and lungs are smaller than males', inhaled irritants become more concentrated. A 2012 study at the Karolinska Institutet in Sweden revealed that there are also differences in proteins produced by immune cells in males and females that may make females more susceptible to lung damage. Further research is under way to determine exactly how these mechanisms influence COPD.

The diagnostic criteria that are now used, including spirometry and other lung-function tests, often do not indicate the presence of COPD until it is well advanced.

In other research on causes, scientists at Brigham and Women's Hospital in Boston are evaluating which genetic factors predispose some smokers to develop COPD. They are studying DNA from smokers who do or do not have COPD to look for gene differences that may increase the risk of COPD or, conversely, may protect some smokers from the disease.

Similar research at Columbia University is assessing whether genes that influence how blood vessels in the lungs respond to smoke play a role in determining whether or not smokers develop COPD. Previous research indicates that a substance called acrolein in cigarette smoke kills cells lining the blood vessels in the lungs and starts the damage that leads to COPD. The researchers believe genetic factors may influence how well these cells withstand the effects of acrolein and are studying smokers' DNA to determine which factors are responsible.

Improving Diagnosis and Disease Staging

Hand-in-hand with efforts to better understand the causes of COPD, researchers are exploring new methods of diagnosing the disease earlier, before major lung damage has occurred. In one study, researchers at Lund University in Sweden are evaluating proteins in the blood of people in different stages of COPD. They are hoping to find proteins that can be used as biomarkers for the various disease stages. Biomarkers are substances in the blood that can be measured and that have been proven to correlate with specific disease types and stages. Thus far, there are no known biomarkers for diagnosing COPD. The diagnostic criteria that are presently used—spirometry and other lung function tests—often do not indicate the presence of COPD until it is well advanced. If researchers identify biomarkers that appear consistently in the early stages of the disease, scientists could then use these biomarkers to develop standardized laboratory tests for early diagnosis. Other biomarkers proven to correlate with later disease stages could be used to diagnose these later stages and also to assess the effectiveness of various treatments.

Scientists at the University of North Carolina–Chapel Hill are conducting similar research to assess whether certain proteins in the blood and urine correlate with FEV1 and other spirometry measurements in people with and without COPD. The Chapel Hill team notes, "The discovery of new treatments for COPD has been slowed by a poor understanding of different types of COPD and a lack of ways to measure whether or not COPD is getting worse."[67] These researchers therefore believe that identifying biomarkers would be beneficial for improving COPD treatment as well as diagnosis.

Given that COPD patients with good lung function (according to spirometry scores) can still experience frequent disease exacerbations, researchers at the University of Zurich in Switzerland also seek to find objective methods of determining whether COPD is worsening. These scientists are developing a risk-assessment score called the age-dyspnea-obstruction index, which they believe will accurately predict a patient's risk of exacerbations and death over a two-to-three year span. The researchers are evaluating data on patients' ability to exercise, lung function, blood chemistry, and quality of life to determine which factors are most important in predicting treatment outcome and patient survival. The researchers write, "After this study, different risk scores will be available for use in primary care so that general practitioners can estimate what impact COPD will have on the patients" and can estimate how "different treatments impact mortality, symptoms, and exacerbations."[68]

New Drugs

Besides seeking to improve treatment through a better understanding of COPD stages, many researchers are developing and testing new treatment drugs. In 2013, QVA149, the first combination long-acting, inhaled bronchodilator that only needs to be taken once per day, was approved for use in Europe and Japan. QVA149 is a combination of the drugs glycopyrronium and indacaterol maleate. Glycopyrronium is an anticholinergic drug originally used to treat stomach ulcers and to relax muscles. Indacaterol maleate is a new beta2-agonist that several recent studies found to be more effective than formoterol and equally effective as tiotropium. Although both glycopyrronium and indacaterol are approved for separate use in the

The PALP™ Device

Along with developing new drugs, researchers are also testing new devices to improve COPD treatment. A study by the medical device manufacturer Maquet Cardiopulmonary AG in Germany is evaluating the safety and effectiveness of a new device called the CO_2-Removal PALP™. PALP stands for "pump-assisted lung protection," and CO_2 is the chemical symbol for carbon dioxide. This device removes carbon dioxide from the blood in patients who are hooked up to a breathing tube due to respiratory failure. It works by draining blood from a vein through a catheter, pumping the blood into a gas-exchange machine that eliminates carbon dioxide, and returning the blood to the patient's body through a vein. The researchers are evaluating whether PALP™ reduces patient death rates, subsequent exacerbations, and the time patients remain on mechanical ventilation.

Previous research reported in 2013 indicates that removing carbon dioxide reduces the time patients stay on mechanical ventilation and helps patients recover faster from these types of COPD exacerbations. However, since the PALP™ concept is very new, the researchers emphasize that "rigorous clinical trials are needed to corroborate these results and to investigate the effect on long-term outcomes and cost effectiveness over conventional management."

Darryl C. Abrams, Keith Brenner, Kristin M. Burkart, Cara L. Agerstrand, Byron M. Thomashow, Matthew Bacchetta, and Daniel Brodie. "Pilot Study of Extracorporeal Carbon Dioxide Removal to Facilitate Extubation and Ambulation in Exacerbations of Chronic Obstructive Pulmonary Disease." *Annals of the American Thoracic Society*, August 2013, p. 307.

United States, QVA149 is not yet approved. Drug manufacturer Novartis is therefore running clinical trials in hopes that the U.S. Food and Drug Administration will approve the combination, which proved to significantly reduce exacerbations and improve lung function and patients' quality of life more than either component taken alone in overseas trials.

Much new drug research is also focused on new and better methods of decreasing lung inflammation. The newer anti-inflammatory drugs are designed to target certain types of white blood cells and the inflammatory chemicals they produce. One promising class of drugs are phosphodiesterase (PDE)-4 inhibitors. PDE-4 is an enzyme that promotes white blood cell activity and the production of inflammatory chemicals. PDE-4 inhibitors block the action of PDE-4 and thus decrease inflammation. However, currently used oral PDE-4 inhibitors like roflumilast have shown limited positive effects because their adverse effects, such as nausea, diarrhea, and weight loss, make them intolerable for many patients. Thus, researchers are testing inhalable PDE-4 inhibitors that seem to have fewer side effects. Studies conducted between 2009 and 2013 in England, Italy, and the Netherlands tested the safety and effectiveness of a new inhaled PDE-4 inhibitor called RPL554 and found it had only mild side effects. RPL554 worked well as a bronchodilator in addition to decreasing inflammation. Further clinical trials are under way.

Another type of anti-inflammatory drug, known as p38 kinase inhibitors, also show promise for COPD treatment. One such drug being tested is PH-797804. It prevents a substance called p38 mitogen-activated protein kinase from activating the inflammatory chemicals interleukin-1, interleukin-6, interleukin-8, and tumor necrosis factor, which all contribute to airway inflammation in COPD. Early clinical trials with PH-797804 indicate that the drug significantly improves lung function and decreases the need for rescue inhalers in people with moderate to severe COPD. Some patients experience mild side effects, but the researchers concluded, "These data are encouraging and support further investigation of the compound in patients with COPD."[69]

Researchers are also testing anti-inflammatory drugs called monoclonal antibodies. Two such drugs being assessed in clinical trials are benralizumab and mepolizumab. These injectable drugs reduce the number of white blood cells known as eosinophils. Large numbers of eosinophils are associated with a high risk of COPD exacerbations. Doctors are now determining which doses of these drugs reduce exacerbations while not dampening patients' immune systems so much that they develop dangerous infections or cancers.

Antismoking Vaccines

Since one of the most important aspects of COPD treatment involves patients' quitting smoking, researchers are also looking for more-effective methods of helping people achieve this goal. Even though existing smoking-cessation drugs help some people quit, many end up starting smoking again after they stop taking the medications. Some scientists believe that a nicotine vaccine may be the answer to this problem. Such a drug would stimulate the body to produce antibodies that stick to nicotine, thus permanently preventing nicotine from entering the brain and exerting its addictive effects. Antibodies are chemicals the immune system produces to specifically destroy or inactivate antigens, or foreign proteins, that enter the body.

Nabi Biopharmaceuticals of Rockville, Maryland, is testing an experimental injectable nicotine vaccine called NicVAX. NicVAX contains a chemical called hapten 3'-aminomethylnicotine that is similar to nicotine and makes the recipient's immune system produce antibodies. These antibodies bind to the nicotine-like substance, creating what are known as antigen-antibody complexes. These complexes are too large to cross the blood-brain barrier (BBB). The BBB is a network of tightly packed cells that prevents many substances in the bloodstream from reaching the all-important central nervous system (the brain and spinal cord). The BBB allows small molecules, such as oxygen and nutrients, to get through but usually prevents larger molecules such as poisons or bacteria from crossing.

Researchers led by Irina Esterlis of Yale University tested NicVAX in smokers and found that 40 percent reduced their use of cigarettes due to reduced nicotine cravings. The researchers also measured the amount of nicotine entering peoples' brains before and after the vaccine was administered, using single-photon emission computed tomography imaging. They found that NicVAX led to a 23.6 percent decrease in the amount of nicotine entering the brain when an individual smoked. Although this is a significant decline, Esterlis states in a Medscape Medical News article that "it appears that vaccination alone may not be the answer to smoking cessation. It is likely that individuals still need cognitive-behavioral support or other pharmaceutical treatment."[70] Other nicotine vaccines are being tested that may lead to better results, and some researchers are testing the effectiveness of combining a nicotine vaccine with drugs like varenicline.

Stem Cell Treatments

Although the goal of nicotine vaccines and most treatment drugs is to slow or stop the progression of COPD, ideally doctors would like to repair the lung damage seen in the disease. Researchers are therefore testing stem cells for this purpose. A promising new field of medicine called regenerative medicine is in fact testing the use of stem cells to repair or replace the damaged cells or tissue that underlie many degenerative diseases.

One study by the Ageless Regenerative Institute is assessing whether transplanting stem cells into COPD patients is safe and effective. Doctors are extracting a small amount of fat from patients, then isolating and removing stem cells from the fat and injecting the stem cells intravenously into the patient from whom they came. Using patients' own cells is important because the immune system would identify cells that come from other people as foreign tissue and destroy them.

Other studies are testing the safety and effectiveness of using mesenchymal stem cells (taken from bone marrow). One study at the Federal Research Clinical Center in Russia is testing whether growing mesenchymal stem cells in the laboratory with limited amounts of oxygen will make the cells more likely to stay alive when transplanted into people with emphysema. In previous studies, cytokines in emphysema patients' lungs killed injected mesenchymal stem cells. The Russian researchers believe that growing these cells with less oxygen will allow them to develop qualities that let them thrive when placed in people with inflamed lungs that deliver less oxygen than normal.

Other research on mesenchymal stem cells has found that when these cells are injected into laboratory rats that have emphysema, the cells migrate to the rats' lungs and develop into

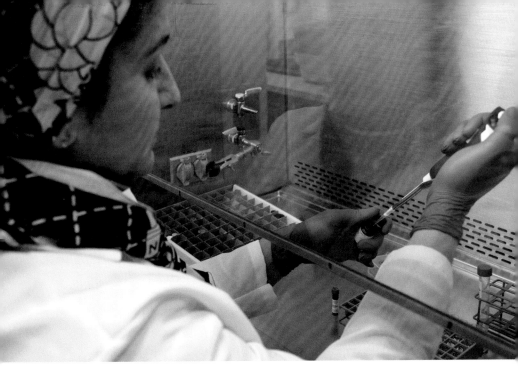

The new field of regenerative medicine is testing the use of stem cells to repair or replace the damaged tissue caused by degenerative diseases such as COPD.

alveolocytes (cells that make up alveoli). Some types of stem cells have shown this capacity when transplanted into humans with certain diseases, but not with COPD as yet. Researchers hope to develop methods of achieving this goal so stem cells can repair or replace damaged alveolar cells and other types of lung cells in people with COPD.

Improving Pulmonary Rehabilitation

Other treatment research is focused on improving patient compliance with various components of PR programs. Many patients have difficulties motivating themselves to do the physical exercise their therapists prescribe because it temporarily increases breathlessness. A study at Uppsala University in Sweden is testing methods of motivating patients to stick with a physical activity regimen. Patients enrolled in the experimental program receive personal counseling from a physiotherapist about the importance of staying active and instructions on how to do so. They also receive motivational telephone calls from counselors to see whether this practice makes them more likely to continue with the program. The researchers write that motivating patients to keep exercising is critical because "the risk of premature morbidity [serious illness] and mortality [death] is especially high in persons with a low level of physical capacity and activity."[71]

A study at Boston's Beth Israel Deaconess Medical Center is testing the effectiveness of motivating patients to exercise in a different way—by offering an exercise program that is easy to do, yet effective. The researchers believe tai chi, an ancient Chinese exercise system that involves slow, flowing motions, may fit these requirements since it has proved to be beneficial for people with a variety of physical and mental disorders. They are assessing COPD patients' willingness to stick with a tai chi program and as a result determining whether tai chi has positive effects on patients' symptoms, strength, lung function, and psychological well-being.

Researchers recommend a physical exercise regimen for COPD patients, but many patients dislike exercising because it temporarily makes breathing even more difficult.

Another study is assessing whether a coping skills program for patients and their caregivers improves patients' attitude, willingness to practice healthy behaviors, and quality of life more than a typical COPD symptom–management education program does. Previous research indicates that anxious, stressed caregivers often lead to a poor attitude and declining lung function in COPD patients. Researchers at Duke University and Ohio State University therefore developed a coping skills training program in which members of the research team offer ongoing advice over the telephone on how patients and caregivers can cope with setbacks, think positively, and pace themselves to avoid becoming physically and mentally exhausted. The researchers also offer assistance with goal setting, planning pleasant and relaxing activities each day, and ways in which patients and caregivers can respectfully communicate their needs and limitations.

Research into Related Conditions

In addition to focusing on improving COPD treatments and treatment compliance, researchers are also addressing methods of reducing other health problems that often go along with COPD. For example, a study sponsored by the North Bristol NHS Trust in England is evaluating why many people with COPD suffer from cognitive impairments. The researchers explain that "moderate to severe cognitive impairment has been shown in up to 60% of certain individuals with COPD and is likely to profoundly influence an individual's ability to manage their disease."[72] The researchers believe the inflammation and oxygen deficiencies that characterize COPD may be leading to capillary damage throughout the body. Capillary damage in the brain is known to cause cognitive impairments, so this study seeks to trace the sequence of events that leads to these problems.

Other researchers believe lung inflammation may contribute to the heart problems many patients experience, particularly during exacerbations and hospitalizations. Doctors at the University of Alberta in Canada are measuring substances in the blood of hospitalized COPD patients that reveal body-wide inflammation to determine whether increases in these substances predict heart problems. The researchers also believe prolonged bed rest in hospitalized patients contributes to the development of heart problems. They are thus studying whether starting patients on a PR program that includes exercise while they are still in the hospital decreases the incidence of heart attacks and other heart problems.

Another major problem for COPD patients is insomnia. Studies show that chronic insomnia quadruples patients' risk of dying from COPD while asleep and significantly increases the risk of frequent disease exacerbations. Yet doctors hesitate

Old Drugs, New Possible Use

One problem with many newer anti-inflammatory drugs being assessed for use in treating COPD is that they reduce inflammation by inhibiting patients' immune systems. This can result in a decreased ability to fight infections and cancers. Other anti-inflammatory drugs that work in different ways may therefore represent less-risky ways of reducing airway inflammation. Two such drugs that are widely used for other purposes are currently being tested for use in COPD.

One of these drugs is the pain, fever, and inflammation reducer acetylsalicylic acid, commonly known as aspirin. Aspirin works by inhibiting the production of chemicals called prostoglandins, which trigger inflammation. Although aspirin can cause stomach upset and ulcers, it does not seem to dampen the immune system in harmful ways. For many years doctors noticed that patients who took aspirin often showed improved lung function. However, aspirin was not tested scientifically for use in COPD until researchers at the Medical University of Vienna began a study that is still ongoing.

The other drugs being tested are statins such as simvastatin. Statins are widely used to lower cholesterol. Coincidently, docto prescribe sleeping pills for COPD patients because these medications affect breathing. Researchers at the University of Illinois–Chicago are therefore studying whether cognitive-behavioral therapy and COPD education help patients sleep better. One cognitive-behavioral intervention involves therapists teaching patients to think about positive things at bedtime so sleep is associated with positive thoughts. The researchers believe that when coupled with COPD education, this therapy "is innovative because it represents a new and substantive departure from the usual insomnia therapy."[73] The usual insomnia therapy consists of medication and/or cognitive-behavior therapy, with no COPD education.

tors began noticing that these drugs also reduce many types of inflammation without harmful side effects. Several research teams are therefore testing the effectiveness of statins in decreasing lung inflammation in COPD patients.

Researchers are testing the cholesterol-lowering drug simvastatin (trade name Zocor) for possible use in reducing the inflammation of the lungs present in COPD patients.

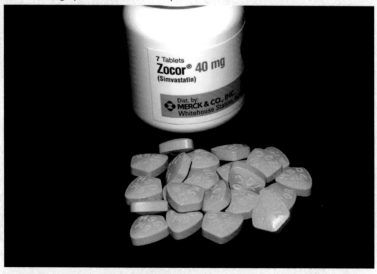

COPD in the Future

With hundreds of studies addressing various aspects of COPD under way, experts believe diagnosis, treatment, awareness, and prevention of the disease will improve in the future. As James Kiley of the National Institutes of Health states in a WebMD article, "We are on a pathway that in 10 years will make things very different for the COPD patient. We hope for novel therapies at a minimum. And at a maximum, would like to say we can regrow lung tissue, repair lung injury, or actually cure COPD. That is a reach, but not totally out of our game plans."[74] However, other experts point out that the future of COPD is not entirely up to doctors and scientists. People at risk must be willing to change behaviors like smoking and being reluctant to seek help so they can reap the benefits of prevention and better treatments. This is partly why COPD advocates continue to promote awareness and outreach campaigns. They hope to convince the public, including patients who may believe they deserve COPD because of their behavior, that those with COPD deserve to benefit from medical advances as much as people with other diseases do.

Notes

Introduction: Shame and Blame

1. Robert Edwards. "Case Statement: Chronic Obstructive Pulmonary Disease (COPD)." Australian Lung Foundation, 2001. www.internationalcopd.org/documents/english /copd_case_statement.pdf.
2. Paula Span. "Fewer Hospitalizations for C.O.P.D. Patients." *The New Old Age* (blog), NYTimes.com, June 28, 2013. http://newoldage.blogs.nytimes.com/2013/06/28 /fewer-hospitalizations-for-c-o-p-d-patients/?_php=true& _type=blogs&_r=2.
3. A.G. Halding, K. Heggdal, and A. Wahl. "Experiences of Self-Blame and Stigmatisation for Self-Infliction Among Individuals Living with COPD." *Scandinavian Journal of Caring Science*, March 2011, p. 100.
4. M. Giacomini, D. DeJean, D. Simeonov, and A. Smith. "Experiences of Living and Dying with COPD." *Ontario Health Technology Assessment Series*, 2012. www.ncbi .nlm.nih.gov/pmc/articles/PMC3384365/#A01ref01.
5. Fabiana Talbot. "Shaming and Blaming." COPD Foundation, March 7, 2014. http://blog.copdfoundation.org /shaming-and-blaming/?utm_source=twitterfeed&utm _medium=twitter.
6. Quoted in Mark A. Earnest. "Explaining Adherence to Supplemental Oxygen Therapy." *Journal of General Internal Medicine*, October 2002, p. 753.
7. Mike McBride. "On to Boston." COPD International, 2009. www.copd-international.com/library/Boston.htm.
8. Quoted in National Heart, Lung, and Blood Institute. "NIH Survey Identifies Barriers to Effective Patient-Provider Dialogue About COPD," November 15, 2013. www.nhlbi .nih.gov/news/press-releases/2013/nih-survey-identifies -barriers-to-effective-patient-provider-dialogue-about -copd.html.

Chapter One: What Is COPD?

9. COPD Foundation. "What Is COPD?," 2014. www.copd foundation.org/What-is-COPD/Understanding-COPD /What-is-COPD.aspx.

10. Qutayba Hamid, Jeanne Shannon, and James Martin. *Physiologic Basis of Respiratory Disease*. Shelton, CT: Peoples' Medical, 2005, p. 85.

11. Quoted in Thomas L. Petty. "The History of COPD." *International Journal of Chronic Obstructive Pulmonary Disease*, March 2006, p. 3.

12. R.T.H. Laënnec. *A Treatise on the Diseases of the Chest*. London: Underwood, 1821, p. 89.

13. Mayo Clinic. "Emphysema." www.mayoclinic.org/diseases -conditions/emphysema/basics/definition/con-20014218.

14. American Thoracic Society. "Chronic Obstructive Pulmonary Disease (COPD)," September 2013. http://patients .thoracic.org/information-series/en/resources/chronic -obstructive-pulmonary-disease-copd.pdf.

15. Susie Bowers. "COPD Is Not a Death Sentence." COPD International, 2004. www.copd-international.com/library /SBowers.htm.

16. Quoted in Alpha-1 Foundation. "Alpha Don Davis Overcomes COPD, Lives a Full Life," 2014. http://alpha-1 foundation.org/davis-overcomes-copd.

17. COPD Foundation. "What Is COPD?"

18. American Lung Association. "Chronic Obstructive Pulmonary Disease," 2008. www.lung.org/assets/documents /publications/lung-disease-data/ldd08-chapters/LDD-08 -COPD.pdf.

19. Quoted in Sandra G. Boodman. "Woman's Labored Breathing Was Not Caused by Allergy, Smoking or Poor Air Quality." *Washington Post*, July 30, 2012. www .washingtonpost.com/national/health-science/womans -labored-breathing-was-not-caused-by-allergy-smoking -or-poor-air-quality/2012/07/30/gJQAJ7nvKX_story.html ?hpid=z5.

20. John Hutchison. "On the Capacity of the Lungs and on the Respiratory Functions, with a View of Establishing a Precise and Easy Method of Detecting Disease by the

Spirometer." *Medico-Chirurgical Transactions*, vol. 29, 1846, p. 154.

21. Jane M. Martin. "End Stage COPD: What Is It and What Does It Mean?" HealthCentral, August 10, 2009. www .healthcentral.com/copd/c/19257/82193/stage-copd.

22. Sundeep Salvi. "Conquering COPD: A Collective Effort." *Express Healthcare*, November 9, 2013. http://healthcare .financialexpress.com/it-healthcare/2144-conquering-copd -a-collective-effort.

23. Global Initiative for Chronic Obstructive Lung Disease. *Global Strategy for the Diagnosis, Management, and Prevention of Chronic Obstructive Pulmonary Disease*, February 7, 2014. www.goldcopd.org/uploads/users/files /GOLD_Report2014_Feb07.pdf.

24. Quoted in Business Wire. "COPD Ranked Third Leading Cause of Death in the U.S., CDC Reports," December 9, 2010. www.businesswire.com/news/home/2010120900 6673/en/COPD-Ranked-Leading-Death-U.S.-CDC-Reports.

Chapter Two: What Causes COPD?

25. Global Initiative for Chronic Obstructive Lung Disease. *Global Strategy for the Diagnosis, Management, and Prevention of Chronic Obstructive Pulmonary Disease*.

26. Graeme P. Currie, ed. *ABC of COPD*. West Sussex, UK: Wiley, 2011, p. 6.

27. Alpha-1 Foundation. "Get Tested," 2014. http://alpha-1 foundation.org/get-tested.

28. Quoted in Weill Cornell Medical College. "Researchers Reveal Link Between COPD Risk Genes and Lung Cells," February 4, 2014. http://weill.cornell.edu/news/news/2014 /02/researchers-reveal-link-between-copd-risk-genes-and -lung-cells.html.

29. Donald P. Tashkin. "Effects of Marijuana Smoking on the Lung." *Annals of the American Thoracic Society*, vol. 10, no. 3, 2013, p. 239.

30. Matthew G. Drake and Christopher G. Slatore. "Smoking Marijuana and the Lungs." *American Journal of Respiratory and Critical Care Medicine*, vol. 187, 2013, p. 5.

31. Canadian Lung Association. "Smoking & Tobacco," September 24, 2012. www.lung.ca/protect-protegez/tobacco -tabagisme/second-secondaire/index_e.php.

32. World Health Organization. "Indoor Air Pollution and Health," September 2011. www.who.int/mediacentre /factsheets/fs292/en.
33. Global Initiative for Chronic Obstructive Lung Disease. *Global Strategy for the Diagnosis, Management, and Prevention of Chronic Obstructive Pulmonary Disease.*
34. Marco Filippone and Eugenio Baraldi. "On Early Life Risk Factors for COPD." *American Journal of Respiratory and Critical Care Medicine*, February 1, 2011, p. 415.
35. C. Svanes et al. "Early Life Origins of Chronic Obstructive Pulmonary Disease." *Thorax*, vol. 65, 2010, pp. 18–19.

Chapter Three: COPD Treatment

36. Canadian Lung Association. "COPD," June 6, 2013. www .lung.ca/diseases-maladies/copd-mpoc/treatment-traite ment/index_e.php.
37. Bunny Music. "Bunny's Story." COPD International, March 22, 2011. www.copd-international.com/library /bunny.htm.
38. Currie. *ABC of COPD*, p. 38.
39. P. Montuschi, F. Macagno, S. Valente, and L. Fuso. "Inhaled Muscarinic Acetylcholine Receptor Antagonists for Treatment of COPD." *Current Medicinal Chemistry*, vol. 20, 2013, p. 1464.
40. François Maltais and Julie Milot. "The Potential for Aclidinium Bromide, a New Anticholinergic, in the Management of Chronic Obstructive Pulmonary Disease." *Therapeutic Advances in Respiratory Disease*, vol. 6, 2012, p. 361.
41. James K. Stoller, Ralph J. Panos, Samuel Krachman, Dennis E. Doherty, Barry Make, and the Long-Term Oxygen Treatment Trial Research Group. "Oxygen Therapy for Patients with COPD." *Chest*, July 2012, p. 180.
42. American Thoracic Society. "Why Do I Need Oxygen Therapy?" www.thoracic.org/clinical/copd-guidelines/for -patients/why-do-i-need-oxygen-therapy.php.
43. National Heart, Lung, and Blood Institute. "What Is Pulmonary Rehabilitation?," August 1, 2010. www.nhlbi.nih .gov/health/health-topics/topics/pulreh.

44. American Thoracic Society. "What Are the Signs and Symptoms of COPD?" www.thoracic.org/clinical/copd -guidelines/for-patients/what-are-the-signs-and-symptoms -of-copd.php.
45. Quoted in Amy Norton. "Diet Tied to Better Breathing in COPD Patients." HealthDay, May 21, 2014. www.nlm.nih .gov/medlineplus/news/fullstory_146384.html.
46. Quoted in Temple University Lung Center. "Double-Lung Transplant Patients Support One Another . . . and Others," May 27, 2014. http://pulmonary.templehealth.org /content/news.htm?inCtx4news_id=54&inCtx4view=24.
47. University of Maryland Medical Center. "Chronic Obstructive Pulmonary Disease," 2014. https://umm.edu/health /medical/altmed/condition/chronic-obstructive-pulmonary -disease.
48. R.D. Martin. *Understanding and Living with COPD*. Rye Brook, NY: Every Breath, 2010, p. 76.

Chapter Four: Living with COPD

49. Currie. *ABC of COPD*, p. 29.
50. Bowers. "COPD Is Not a Death Sentence."
51. Quoted in Boodman. "Woman's Labored Breathing Was Not Caused by Allergy, Smoking or Poor Air Quality."
52. Vera Franks. "Personal Side of Living with COPD." Emphysema Foundation for Our Right to Survive, October 17, 2007. www.emphysema.net/patient_stories.htm#Vera _Franks.
53. Martin. *Understanding and Living with COPD*, p. 19.
54. Bowers. "COPD Is Not a Death Sentence."
55. Quoted in Gunilla Lindqvist and Lillemor Hallberg. "'Feelings of Guilt Due to Self-Inflicted Disease': A Grounded Theory of Suffering from Chronic Obstructive Pulmonary Disease (COPD)." *Journal of Health Psychology*, vol. 15, no. 3, 2010, p. 461.
56. Ian Wilson. "Depression in the Patient with COPD." *International Journal of Chronic Obstructive Pulmonary Disease*, March 2006, p. 61.
57. Martin. *Understanding and Living with COPD*, p. 13.
58. Quoted in Alpha-1 Foundation. "Roger and What's 'Just Out of Reach.'" 2014. http://alpha-1foundation.org/roger -and-whats-just-out-of-reach.

59. Music. "Bunny's Story."
60. Martin. *Understanding and Living with COPD*, p. 115.
61. Quoted in Alpha-1 Foundation. "Alpha Don Davis Overcomes COPD, Lives a Full Life."
62. Martin M. Shenkman. *Estate and Financial Planning for People Living with COPD*. New York: Demos Medical, 2013, p. 134.
63. Quoted in Alpha-1 Foundation. "Michelle's Photos Tell All—Alpha-1 Doesn't Get in Her Way," March 20, 2012. http://alpha-1foundation.org/michelles-photos-tell-all-alpha -1-doesnt-get-in-her-way.

Chapter Five: The Future

64. COPD Foundation. "CME Credits," 2014. www.copd foundation.org/Learn-More/For-Medical-Professionals /CME-Credits.aspx.
65. World Health Organization. "Chronic Obstructive Pulmonary Disease," October 2013. www.who.int/mediacentre /factsheets/fs315/en.
66. World Health Organization. "Indoor Air Pollution and Health."
67. University of North Carolina–Chapel Hill. "Study of COPD Subgroups and Biomarkers (SPIROMICS)." Clinical Trials.gov, April 2014. https://clinicaltrials.gov/ct2/show/NCT 01969344?term=copd&rank=209.
68. University of Zurich. "Predicting the Course of Chronic Obstructive Pulmonary Disease (COPD) in Primary Care." Clinical Trials.gov, June 2010. https://clinicaltrials.gov/ct2 /show/NCT00706602?term=copd&rank=244.
69. William MacNee, Richard J. Allan, Ieuan Jones, Maria Cristina De Salvo, and Lisa F. Tan. "Efficacy and Safety of the Oral P38 Inhibitor PH-797804 in Chronic Obstructive Pulmonary Disease." *Thorax*, vol. 68, 2013. www.medscape .com/viewarticle/807722_4.
70. Quoted in Megan Brooks. "Nicotine Vaccine Promising for Smoking Cessation." Medscape Medical News, February 26, 2013. www.medscape.com/viewarticle/779915.
71. Uppsala University. "Behavioral Intervention to Maintain Physical Capacity and Activity in Patients with Chronic

Obstructive Pulmonary Disease (COPD)." Clinical Trials
.gov, February 2012. http://clinicaltrials.gov/ct2/show
/study/NCT01539434?term=copd&rank=16.

72. North Bristol NHS Trust. "Novel Vascular Manifestations
of Chronic Obstructive Pulmonary Disease." Clinical Trials
.gov, February 2014. https://clinicaltrials.gov/ct2/show
/NCT02060292?term=copd&rank=32.

73. University of Illinois–Chicago. "A Behavioral Therapy for
Insomnia Co-existing with COPD." Clinical Trials.gov, July
2014. https://clinicaltrials.gov/ct2/show/NCT01973647
?term=copd&rank=35.

74. Quoted in Daniel J. DeNoon. "COPD Prognosis." WebMD,
September 12, 2012. www.webmd.com/lung/copd/features
/copd-prognosis?page=2.

Glossary

alpha-1 antitrypsin deficiency: A genetic condition that can cause COPD.

alveoli: Air sacs in the lungs that transfer oxygen into the bloodstream and remove carbon dioxide from the bloodstream.

anthracotic: Blackened lungs from coal or smoke.

augmentation therapy: Treatment for alpha-1 COPD that increases the amount of alpha-1 antitrypsin protein in the body.

biomarkers: Chemicals in the blood that can be used to diagnose or stage different diseases.

bronchi: The body's breathing tubes or airways.

bronchitis: Inflammation of the airways; chronic bronchitis is one of the conditions that occur in people with COPD.

bronchodilator: A drug that relaxes muscles in the airways.

bullae: Air-filled blisters in the lungs that occur in people with emphysema.

COPD: Chronic obstructive pulmonary disease.

dyspnea: Breathlessness or shortness of breath.

emphysema: One of the conditions involved in COPD; emphysema results from destruction of alveoli in the lungs.

exacerbation: Worsening of symptoms.

genes: The parts of DNA molecules that encode instructions to body cells.

hypercapnia: An increased amount of carbon dioxide in the blood.

pulmonary: Referring to the lungs and breathing system.

pulmonologist: A physician who specializes in lung diseases.

respiratory: Related to breathing.

spirometer: A device used to measure how well an individual is breathing.

trachea: Windpipe.

Organizations to Contact

Alpha-1 Foundation

3300 Ponce de Leon Blvd.
Coral Gables, FL 33134
(305) 567-9888
http://alpha-1foundation.org

The Alpha-1 Foundation is a nonprofit organization that shares information about alpha-1 antitrypsin deficiency, promotes research, and seeks to better the lives of people affected by this condition.

American College of Chest Physicians

CHEST Global Headquarters
2595 Patriot Blvd.
Glenview, IL 60026
(224) 521-9800
www.chestnet.org

The American College of Chest Physicians is a professional organization that helps educate and train doctors who specialize in lung diseases. Its website has extensive information about all aspects of COPD.

American Lung Association

55 W. Wacker Dr., Ste. 1150
Chicago, IL 60601
(800) 586-4872
www.lung.org

The American Lung Association is an organization dedicated to improving lung health and preventing lung disease. It provides information about all aspects of COPD, including causes, prevention, diagnosis, treatment, research, and patient support.

American Thoracic Society

25 Broadway, 18th Fl.
New York, NY 10004
(212) 315-8600
www.thoracic.org

The American Thoracic Society is an organization of health care professionals who specialize in respiratory diseases. Its website provides extensive information about all aspects of COPD.

Centers for Disease Control and Prevention (CDC)

1600 Clifton Rd.
Atlanta, GA 30333
(800) 232-4636
www.cdc.gov

The CDC is a government agency that tracks health trends and provides public information and statistics on all aspects of diseases, including COPD.

COPD Foundation

Development, Communications and
Public Policy Departments
20 F St. NW, Ste. 200-A
Washington, DC 20001
(866) 731-2673
www.copdfoundation.org

The COPD Foundation is a nonprofit organization that seeks to improve the lives of people with COPD through education, advocacy, research, and support. It provides information about all aspects of the disease.

COPD International

131 DW Hwy. #627
Nashua, NH 03060
www.copd-international.com

COPD International is a nonprofit organization that provides information and support for people affected by COPD. Its website contains information about all aspects of COPD and living with the disease.

National Emphysema Foundation (NEF)

128 East Ave.
Norwalk, CT 06851
(203) 866-5000
www.emphysemafoundation.org

The NEF is a nonprofit organization that seeks to educate the public and emphysema patients about emphysema and COPD. Its website provides information about causes, treatment, prevention, research, and living with COPD.

National Heart, Lung, and Blood Institute (NHLBI)

Health Information Center
PO Box 30105
Bethesda, MD 20824
(301) 592-8573
www.nhlbi.nih.gov

The NHLBI is a branch of the National Institutes of Health that sponsors research and educates the public about heart, lung, and blood disorders. It provides comprehensive information about all aspects of COPD.

World Health Organization

Avenue Appia 20
1211 Geneva 27
Switzerland
+41 22 791 21 11
www.who.int

WHO is the United Nations' health authority. It provides information, sets worldwide standards, and promotes international solutions for diseases and health issues, including COPD.

For More Information

Books

Carol Ballard. *Lungs*. Mankato, MN: Heinemann-Raintree, 2009. Written for teens, this book discusses the structure, function, and importance of the lungs and respiratory system.

Beverly Cordes. *Breathing for Life: As We Breathe, We Hope*. Bloomington, IN: AuthorHouse, 2012. This book shares the inspiring personal stories of people living with respiratory diseases such as COPD.

Daniel E. Harmon. *Pollution and Your Lungs*. New York: Rosen, 2013. This book is written for teens and discusses the effects of environmental pollutants on the lungs.

Sarah Levete. *Understanding the Heart, Lungs, and Blood*. New York: Rosen, 2010. This book explores how the heart, lungs, and blood function and interact in the human body.

Judy Monroe Peterson. *Breathe: Keeping Your Lungs Healthy*. New York: Rosen Central, 2012. Written for teens; discusses how the lungs work, how to keep them healthy, and how they respond to smoking and other irritants.

Internet Sources

COPD International. "Chrissy's Story." www.copdinternatio nal.com/teensplace/Chrissy.htm.

TeensHealth from Nemours. "Lungs and Respiratory System." http://kidshealth.org/teen/your_body/body_basics/lungs .html#cat20121.

TeensHealth from Nemours. "Secondhand Smoke." http://kid shealth.org/teen/your_body/take_care/secondhand_smoke .html#cat20116.

Websites

Be Tobacco Free, US Department of Health and Human Services (http://betobaccofree.hhs.gov). This website provides links to extensive information and guidance about the effects of smoking, how to quit, and how not to start.

COPD, Mayo Clinic (www.mayoclinic.org/diseases-conditions /copd/basics/definition/CON-20032017). The Mayo Clinic website offers easily understood information on symptoms, causes, risk factors, diagnoses, coping, treatment, and prevention of COPD.

Smoke Free Teen (http://teen.smokefree.gov). This U.S. government website seeks to educate teens about smoking and its effects.

What Is COPD?, National Heart, Lung, and Blood Institute (www.nhlbi.nih.gov/health/health-topics/topics/copd). This US government website gives an understandable overview of how the lungs work and how COPD affects the respiratory system.

Index

Picture Credits

About the Author

Melissa Abramovitz has been a writer for more than twenty-five years and specializes in writing nonfiction magazine articles and books for all age groups. She is the author of hundreds of magazine articles, more than forty educational books for children and teenagers, numerous poems and short stories, several children's picture books, and a book for writers. She holds a degree in psychology from the University of California–San Diego and is a graduate of the Institute of Children's Literature.